W9-BPM-057

(Continued)

WINDOWS ON LEARNING

Documenting Young Children's Work

Judy Harris Helm
Sallee Beneke
Kathy Steinheimer

FOREWORD BY LILIAN G. KATZ

Teachers College, Columbia University
New York and London

Published by Teachers College Press, 1234 Amsterdam Avenue, New York, NY 10027

Library of Congress Cataloging-in-Publication Data
Helm, Judy Harris.
    Windows on learning : documenting young children's work / Judy Harris Helm,
Sallee Beneke, Kathy Steinheimer.
        p.   cm.   — (Early childhood education series)
    Includes bibliographical references and index.
    ISBN 0-8077-3679-1 (cloth: alk. Paper). — ISBN 0-8077-3678-3 (pbk.: alk. Paper)
    1. Project method in teaching. 2. Early childhood education — Documentation.
3. Portfolios in education. 4. School reports. I. Beneke, Sallee. II. Steinheimer, Kathy.
III. Title. IV. Series: Early childhood education series (Teachers College Press)
LB1139.35.P8H45 1997
372.13′6—dc21   97-40770

ISBN 0-8077-3678-3 (paper)
ISBN 0-8077-3679-1 (cloth)

Printed on acid-free paper

Manufactured in the United States of America

05 04 03 02 01   8 7 6 5

DEDICATION

From Judy: To my family—Rich, Amanda, Rebecca, and my parents.

From Sallee: To my husband, Bill, and my children, Maggie, Alice, Tommy, and Abby.

From Kathy: To my mom, John, Sally, Sue, Martha, Timothy, and the memory of my dad.

Contents

Foreword

"What happened in school today?" Even though this important question is a simple one, it is surprisingly difficult to provide meaningful answers. In this book, Judy Helm, Sallee Beneke and Kathy Steinheimer present a practical approach to answering the question by making the experiences of the children in early childhood classrooms visible and understandable to the participants as well as those not present.

The suggestions and guidelines are presented with clear step-by-step explanations and examples based on the authors' rich experiences of working with teachers and children throughout Illinois in schools, university laboratory schools, child care centers, and the innovative Valeska-Hinton Early Childhood Center in Peoria. Based on their own firsthand experience, ideas, and insights, the authors share their approach to the challenge of how all those who have a stake in an early childhood program can come to know and appreciate what happened in school today, yesterday, and the day before through what has come to be called *documentation*.

Teacher observations and anecdotal records have always been recommended as a way to enhance teaching, learning, and knowledge in early childhood education. Indeed, a substantial body of literature has been available for many decades on the value of careful observation of children at work and play in preschool and kindergarten classes.

The current term documentation, of which traditional observation techniques are a part, further advances the traditional approaches by adding in the modern technologies of video- and audio-taping and especially of making the observations in various media readily visible to all interested in the experiences of the children. In this context, a document is a narrative record of events including photos, drawings, transcribed audiotapes of discussions and comments, videotapes, captions and much more.

Renewed interest in documentation and deeper appreciation of how it can enlighten all concerned is due in very large part to our colleagues in Reggio Emilia, Italy. We are especially grateful to them for setting new standards of early childhood education in both the quality of documentation and the quality of the children's experiences being documented.

Helm, Beneke, and Steinheimer, working in the heart of the United States with a very diverse population of children and families help us to realize that the practice of documenting the children's thoughts, ideas, and work can contribute to the quality of an early childhood program in several ways. Through involvement in the processes of preparing the documentaries of their work, children re-visit and reflect on their experience in ways that yield new and deeper understandings of what they have been studying. Through documentation parents can become intimately and deeply aware of their children's experience in the school, and particularly of their increasing knowledge and skillfulness. Documentation can also help to alert teachers to the children's understandings and misunderstandings, their developing skills, and aspects of their growth with which they need assistance, thereby allowing teachers to make informed decisions about how best to support each child's development.

Narrative documentation also provides teachers and parents with insight into the children's thought processes during their work that cannot be seen from merely viewing final products.

Finally, documentation provides information about children's learning and progress that cannot be revealed by traditional formal standardized tests and checklists. While teachers often gain important information from their own firsthand observations, the documentation of children's work provides compelling public evidence of the intellectual powers of young children that is not available in any other way that I know of.

As the authors of this very welcome volume make clear, the powerful contribution of documentation is possible in part because the children are engaged in complex, interesting projects and activities worthy of documentation. Teachers using the book will be able to create windows for their own viewing of the complex and dynamic events in their classrooms and to help the children and parents to appreciate them, too.

Lilian G. Katz
University of Illinois

Acknowledgments

The authors wish to thank the contributions made by the following people to this work:

Lilian Katz, who mentored and encouraged us as we investigated this topic, and who provided invaluable criticism and advice in the first drafts of this book; Sylvia Chard, for providing insight through her writing and teaching; Ken Hinton, director of Valeska Hinton Early Childhood Education Center, for inspiration and support; the teachers of Valeska Hinton Early Childhood Education Center, whose work is included in this book; Stacy Berg, Jolyn Blank, Suzi Boos, Monica Borrowman, Anna Brown, Rachel Bystry, Judy Cagle, Beth Crider-Olcott, Michelle Didesch, MaryAnn Gottlieb, Gail Gordon, Renee Jackson, Valerie McCall, Pam Scranton, Tammy Shinkey, and Valerie Timmes; Illinois Valley Community College Early Childhood Education Center Director Diane Christianson, teacher Rebecca Tonellie, and student teachers Ellen Bejster, Mindy Kramer, Theresa Leifheit, Linda Petelin, Arin Sorenson, and Robyn Tonelli; teachers Mary Jane Elliott, Don Shuler, Lee Makovichuk, and Kim Fisher, who also shared their work; Dr. Maxine Wortham and Mary Ann Randle for encouraging us to persevere in getting our thoughts on paper and smoothing the way for sharing the children's work; Paula Ellberg for her feedback; Char Ward and the staff of STARNET at Western Illinois University, for their early recognition of our research and their encouragement; Susan Liddicoat for her calm and thoughtful editing; Peter Sieger for his patience and persistence in editing our photos and children's work; and most of all to the children and their parents who allowed us to share their stories.

Introduction

A visitor coming into the school for the first time is stopped by the children's work hanging on the walls. Drawings, paintings, and plans, carefully displayed in pleasing arrangements, attract his attention. A title tells the visitor that children are studying "The Pond." A large mural of a pond covers one wall. The visitor first admires the mural as children's art. Leaning closer, he is struck by the detail and care with which each element of the mural has been executed. Around the mural, he sees preliminary sketches of sections of the mural. Photographs show children sitting by a pond and in a meadow sketching the very plans that he now sees displayed.

The visitor is captivated by the look on the face of a child searching for information in a book. The child is intently involved in her work. Her small finger is on the picture in her book, and her small clipboard with her notes lies next to the book. The visitor can see that the child is comparing the picture in the book with her own drawing. The teacher's notes explain that the child is using books as a resource for the first time. As the visitor looks at the picture he notices how very small the child is. Quickly searching the wall, he finds a summary written on a printed form and framed. "These children are 5 years old!" He wonders, "How did these children learn so much about the pond? How did they acquire the skills to do this kind of work?"

The visitor hears children coming down the hall. Peering down the corridor, he sees a small group of children settling onto the floor facing another display of children's work. They are carrying papers with them of work they have done. As he watches, he hears them discussing the work that they had previously completed, which is now displayed on the wall. The children are comparing the work on the wall to their latest work and talking about what they now know that they did not know before. The teacher is jotting notes on a Post-it pad and sticking the notes on a clipboard. Next to the notes she is making a list on a page entitled "Books and Materials Needed."

Turning the corner of the hall, the visitor almost stumbles over a large block structure of a water treatment plant. Labels made by the children designate the primary and secondary treatment pools. Having learned from his first experience with the mural, he immediately searches the walls to find the summary of this project. He sees that this study lasted 3 weeks and was completed by 3- and 4-year-olds. He also notices that this display includes teacher observations of how individual children's concepts changed.

As he enters the office to conduct his business, his first comment to the secretary is, "I can see that children are really learning at this school!"

This book grew out of the experiences of teachers at schools like the one just described as they learned to document young children's work. The schools range from a comprehensive, state-of-the-art early intervention center in an urban setting, to a small school in a small town on the Mississippi River, to a community college laboratory school. Their path to documenting followed several routes. Some learned first to use an authentic assessment system, some learned how to use the project approach and document that process, and some learned how to document as they first learned how to teach in a teacher preparation program. What they had in common was wanting to know how to teach better, how to meet the needs of their children, and how to open the eyes of others to the wonderful world of young children's learning.

We shared that experience intimately with some of them. As a teacher, a lead teacher, and a teacher educator, we were involved in the experimentation, teaching children, asking questions, observing, applying, arguing, and reflecting. We developed frameworks to help us all understand, and we reworked and reworded those frameworks until they began to take a form that could support our ideas and serve as a foundation for our thinking about documenting children's learning. With some of the teachers in this book, we connected briefly but with great enthusiasm as they shared with us their own experimentations and what they learned. We read widely and incorporated the work of many others, building on their pioneering efforts and using their points of view to enrich our own. We are grateful to those who came before us and took the time to write down what they had learned. You will see their remarks quoted throughout this book. The one thing all of these teachers shared was an interest in learning how to document, to make it part of their teaching strategies.

USING AN AUTHENTIC ASSESSMENT SYSTEM

Our first experience with documenting children's work was through the use of an authentic assessment system. Many teachers whose work is shared in this book use an authentic assessment system, with most using the Work Sampling System, summarized in Appendix A (Meisels et al., 1994). The Work Sampling System is a performance assessment that provides an alternative to group-administered, norm-referenced achievement tests in preschool through fifth grade. Its purpose "is to document and assess children's skills, knowledge, behavior, and accomplishments across a wide variety of [curriculum] on multiple occasions" (p. 4). The Work Sampling System consists of three complementary components: (1) developmental guidelines and checklists, (2) portfolios of children's work, and (3) summary reports completed by teachers.

Assessments based on the Work Sampling approach take place three times a year. They are designed to reflect classroom goals and objectives and to help teachers keep track of children's continuous progress by placing their work within a broad, developmental perspective. Through its focus on documenting individual performance of classroom-based tasks, Work Sampling enhances student motivation, assists teachers in instructional decision making, and serves as an effective means for reporting children's progress to families, professional educators, and the community (Meisels et al., 1994).

The Work Sampling System provided us not only a framework for systematically collecting and processing children's work but also an understanding of how to observe, how to collect, and how to analyze. It enabled us to set up a plan so that we sampled all children's work in all areas of development. It also provided a systematic way to collect, store, and organize the portfolios. Through the training process, we learned about nonbiased and nonjudgmental observing and recording of behavior. The checklist gave us a comprehensive and developmentally appropriate picture of what children can be expected to know and do across all domains of growth and learning. Especially valuable to the development of documentation skills was the collection and rating schedule that paced the teachers through the process and provided an impetus for ongoing, systematic collection of children's work.

UNDERSTANDING THE PROJECT APPROACH

About half of the teachers in this book participated in a class with Lilian Katz on the project approach. These teachers incorporated their knowledge about collecting, observing, and recording that they had gained through applying the assessment system to the task of adding the project approach to their curriculum.

The project approach is a good example of developmentally appropriate, active, engaging, and meaningful learning. A project is an in-depth study, over an extended period of time, of a topic that is of high interest to an individual, a small group, or a whole class (Katz & Chard, 1989). Skills and concepts are learned by children through their efforts to find answers to questions about a topic. Topics are posed by either the children, the teacher, or the teacher working with the children. Independent and group planning, construction, research, and representation are all ways that children learn in the project approach.

The project approach is similar to thematic teaching in its integrated approach to content but is different in the emphasis on child investigation and problem solving. Children become emotionally involved in the learning experience. The project approach is not new in education, but interest has been revived and extended by the changes in understanding of how children learn and the need to develop problem-solving skills in order to meet the challenges of a technological society.

Doing projects is an approach with great promise for all children. Helping parents and community members to see the value of this approach depends upon the teacher's ability to provide comprehensive, good-quality documentation of what children are doing and learning. Careful and systematic recording of learning can enable the teacher to meet accountability needs while using this promising approach. Documentation can capture for the teacher, the parent, the school administration, and the public a vision of the intellectual development that occurs while children are involved in research. They can also see the strengthening of the variety of intellectual and social dispositions that occurs while the children work together, argue, hypothesize, and predict. Documentation enables the teacher to monitor the development of the project. It is a method of evaluating and improving the project as the project develops.

As we incorporated the project approach into our curriculum, some of the benefits of documentation that we were seeking started to occur. A good example is seen in these comments from Chuck Fabish, assistant regional superintendent of schools in Peoria County, Illinois. Mr. Fabish, a former physics teacher, had visited a school where documentation of a project on "Reflections" was displayed.

> I was intrigued by their level of conceptual understanding. By utilizing their walk-in kaleidoscope, they were able to predict the effect that modifying the angle of the mirrors had on the resulting number of "pictures" (images). Additionally, these children were adept at explaining practical reflection applications and incidental reflectors such as spoons, water, aluminum foil. In some respects, they had a better "feel" for reflection than some of my former physics students.

As the teachers began to collect and display documentation of the projects, we, as professional development coordinator and lead teacher at Valeska Hinton Early Childhood Education Center, sought a framework or an image upon which to focus our discussion and reflection about documentation. The first image that we developed and shared with staff at the Center was the framework of the windows described in Chapter 2. The second image was the Types of Documentation Web described in Chapter 3, which shows a variety of ways to document. The web and its pieces, which appear throughout the book, provided an impetus to document in many different ways. We began collecting examples of documentation. As teachers from other programs also learned to do projects, their input and their examples were also added to the web. Discussions about documentation and extensive reading provided the ideas for organizing and presenting documentation.

We soon discovered that it was in the careful documentation of children's learning in the project approach that teachers were most able to meet the needs for assessment and program evaluation without narrowing children's experiences. The project approach enriched and increased the complexity of the items that teachers were able to collect in an authentic assessment process. Work samples that resulted from project work were more informative than work samples collected when children were doing teacher-directed learning activities.

Documentation of children's learning occurred throughout the day at most of these schools, not just during the time children were working on projects; but it was in the project work that the value of active, engaged learning was so dramatically demonstrated through documentation.

LEARNING ABOUT THE REGGIO EMILIA SCHOOLS

One of the reasons that interest has grown in the project approach is the demonstration of high-quality early childhood education in the schools of Reggio Emilia in Italy. These schools also use projects extensively and have been extremely successful in demonstrating the wealth of knowledge and skills that are gained in these projects through their use of aesthetically displayed documentation. Forman, Lee, Wrisley, and Langley (1993) discuss the relationship between projects and documentation:

> Documentation and time to study the documentation are essential for a successful project. This is perhaps the first priority in Reggio Emilia, with great emphasis placed on the time to study the documentation. . . . If done properly, good documentation can serve all masters simultaneously, from individual assessment, to curriculum planning, to instructional accountability. (p. 249)

When we began our study of documentation and developed the windows framework and the documentation web, we knew very little about the Reggio Emilia schools. After we had been working on combining the project approach and our authentic assessment system for documentation, we visited "The Hundred Languages of Children," the touring exhibit from Reggio Emilia.

We were impressed by the displays and the quality of children's work. Our interest in documentation intensified, and we read extensively about the Reggio Emilia schools (Edwards, Gandini, & Forman, 1993; Katz, 1990; New, 1990, 1991; Rankin, 1992) and attended conference presentations on the topic. Almost 2 years after first beginning to study documentation, we visited the Reggio Emilia schools in Italy during the 1996 Summer Institute. We were inspired by the environments and the commitment of the staff. At the same time, although we had been cautioned about the differences between our culture and the culture of Reggio Emilia, we were surprised at how great the differences were and how our approach to documentation, as it had evolved, differed from theirs. We came home with strong commitments to redefine our own image of the child, explore the hundred languages, persevere in our exploration of projects, develop more flexible time, and take more time to reflect.

The documentation that takes place in the schools of Reggio Emilia is extensive and rich. According to Lella Gandini (1993), documentation in these schools has several functions:

> To make parents aware of their children's experiences and maintain parental involvement; to allow teachers to understand children better and to evaluate the teachers' own work, thus promoting their professional growth; to facilitate communication and exchange of ideas among educators; to make children aware that their effort is valued; and to create an archive that traces the history of the school and of the pleasure and process of learning by many children and their teachers. (p. 8)

All of these functions are similar to the functions of documentation in our schools. However, according to founder Loris Malaguzzi (1993), the schools of Reggio Emilia

> have no planned curriculum with units and subunits. . . . Instead every year each school delineates a series of related projects, some short range and some long. These themes serve as the main structural supports, but then it is up to the children, the course of events, and the teachers to determine whether the building turns out to be a hut on stilts, or an apartment house or whatever. (p. 85)

Although we at times envied the staff of the schools of Reggio Emilia their ability to so freely follow the lead of the children, we found that was more difficult to do in our schools. Following developmentally appropriate practices, "teachers make plans to enable children to attain key curriculum goals across various disciplines such as language arts, mathematics, social studies, science, art, music, physical education, and health" (Bredekamp & Copple, 1997, p. 18). In many schools in our educational systems, there are state learning goals, standardized achievement tests, exit exams, or required public disclosure by program, school, or district of student performance. Even teachers in private preschool programs without governmental requirements are often challenged to demonstrate their effectiveness. In addition, parents often have content expectations and share these when participating in goal setting for early childhood programs. These factors resulted in more emphasis on accountability in our documentation.

For a program to succeed, or a teacher to succeed, it is important that the teacher be able to provide evidence of how the learning occurring in the classroom relates to goals and objectives of the district or program. Even teachers with few restrictions on how they teach are often frustrated when they are unable to articulate to others the value of active, engaged, and meaningful learning experiences such as the project approach. We found that documentation enabled us to see children's learning more clearly, allowing us to more easily integrate content into emergent curriculum approaches. Documentation also enabled us to help others understand how emergent curriculum approaches can be an effective way to meet content goals.

Many of our teachers face the challenges of high mobility of both children and staff and an increase in the number of children in poverty. On our visit to Reggio Emilia, we were reminded of our differences when we learned about the family and economic stability in Reggio. Being involved with programs for children at risk, we know it is important to closely monitor each child's development. This does not mean focusing on children's deficits but rather identifying strengths, maximizing teaching effectiveness, and accessing resources as needed. This positive focus resulted in documentation that included systematic collections of each child's work in each area of learning in addition to the documentation of the projects.

One lesson that we learned in Reggio Emilia was the immense power of documentation. The schools themselves, which are paid for by the city of Reggio Emilia, are a tribute to the ability of the staff to involve the families and the community. Their consistent, informative, high-quality documentation has, no doubt, contributed greatly to that involvement. We were inspired to persist in our exploration of documentation and to adapt many of the documentation processes of Reggio Emilia to our own schools.

INTRODUCING OUR SCHOOLS

Examples in this book are drawn from many different schools. However, two schools were instrumental in the development of our concept of documentation. The Valeska Hinton Early Childhood Education Center is a public school early childhood program in Peoria, Illinois. It provides a comprehensive full-day, year-round program for children ages 3 through 6. The center is divided into four villages, or minischools, of five classrooms each. Children enter a village and stay in that village for 4 years. The children are with one teaching team in a village when they are 3 and 4 years old, then with another teaching team within the same village when they are 5 and 6 years old. The villages are named for the primary colors—red, yellow, blue, and green. Teachers in each village meet weekly to plan and reflect. Seventy-five percent of the children at Valeska Hinton Early Childhood Education Center come from low-income families. We worked at the Center as professional development coordinator, lead teacher, and teacher.

Illinois Valley Community College is the other site where extensive experimentation and development of the documentation concepts presented in this book occurred. This small, rural community college in the north-central part of the state offers a 2-year child development degree. An on-campus child-care center functions as a laboratory for practicum students who are learning how to teach and an exemplary center for area child-care programs.

Other schools are represented in this book by teachers who have shared their knowledge and experiences with documentation with us through workshops, conferences, and the Internet. By writing this book, we hope to expand this network by encouraging more teachers to adopt the practice of documenting young children's learning.

OVERVIEW OF THIS BOOK

Part I of this book enables readers to learn about documentation. Chapter 1 provides the rationale for the study of documentation. In Chapter 2, readers will find the windows framework for thinking about documentation that guided the teachers. In Chapter 3, the web of types of documentation is introduced. Chapters 4–8 provide an in-depth exploration of the variety of types of documentation, with samples collected by the teachers. Through children's work and teacher notes, readers will see what children learned and how they developed through use of the project approach.

In Part II, Chapters 9–11, readers will learn how to collect, organize, and share documentation with children, other teachers, parents, and the community. Throughout the book and especially in Chapter 10, teacher reflections will show readers how the teachers used documentation to inform teaching and make decisions. In Chapter 11 readers will learn how documentation as described in this book relates to recommendations and requirements for assessment.

Part III takes readers through the documentation of one project, "Our Mail Project," which was completed by a class of 3- and 4-year-olds over a 6-week time period. Through the teacher's and the children's documentation, readers will experience the progress of "Our Mail Project" as it grew, expanded, and concluded. Each type of documentation carries labels from the web to help readers relate this example to the concepts explained in the earlier chapters of the book. The complete documentation of this project will assist readers in understanding how a project develops, how documentation can be integrated into all areas of development, how documentation informs teaching, and how documentation enables others to see how much learning occurred in the classroom.

* * *

Two additional resources for teachers wishing to implement the ideas that are presented in this book are available from Teachers College Press. The first is *Teacher Materials for Documenting Young Children's Work: Using Windows on Learning*, a companion to *Windows on Learning* that provides forms for thinking about documentation, forms for collecting and analyzing what occurs in the classroom, lists of materials and supplies, handouts for parents, and sample display layouts. The second is an 20-minute video, *Windows on Learning: A Framework for Making Decisions*, that brings to life—through animation and classroom vignettes—the documentation web and the process of documentation. Filmed at Valeska Hinton Early Childhood Education Center, it shows on the walls of the school many of the examples discussed in this book. Kathy Steinheimer, the teacher in "Our Mail Project," which is featured in this book, is shown documenting in the classroom. She and coauthor Sallee Beneke reflect on journaling and the process of learning to document.

PART I

Learning About Documentation

CHAPTER 1

The Value of Documentation

document: —2. To support (an assertion or a claim, for example) with evidence or decisive information.

—American Heritage Dictionary (1994)

Documenting children's learning may be one of the most valuable skills a teacher can develop today. A teacher who perceives how children learn and can then help others to see the learning can contribute significantly to the child's development. The visitor to the school described at the beginning of the Introduction said, "I can see that these children are learning." He was able to see what the children were learning because teachers had carefully collected, analyzed, interpreted, and displayed the evidence. This use of documentation is directly related to what research in the early childhood field has demonstrated about how children learn.

APPLYING WHAT IS KNOWN ABOUT CHILDREN'S LEARNING

Many early childhood teachers are aware of the literature on the importance of active, engaged, meaningful learning experiences and the importance of children's constructing their own knowledge through interaction with their environments and with others (Berk & Winsler, 1995; Gardner, 1991; Kamii & Ewing, 1996; Katz & Chard, 1989; Vygotsky, 1978). The work of Piaget (Devries & Kohlberg, 1990; Kamii, 1982; Kamii & Ewing, 1996) demonstrates the importance of sensory experiences and concrete learning activities. The National Association for the Education of Young Children confirmed the importance of direct, first-hand, interactive experience in the position statement, *Developmentally Appropriate Practices* (Bredekamp, 1987), and reconfirmed it in the revised and updated version (Bredekamp & Copple, 1997).

Early childhood teachers are also aware of the importance of providing opportunities to develop positive dispositions toward learning, a concept described by Bruner (1996), Katz (1985, 1987), and Smith (1990). Dispositions are "relatively enduring habits of mind or action, or tendencies to respond to categories of experience across classes of situations" (Katz, 1985, p. 1). Dispositions are preferences of what we choose to think about (Smith, 1990).

> We are all disposed to think about some things but not about others—depending on our interest in them, and whether we feel they are within our competence . . . the disposition to think about particular matters rises and falls on the tides of positive and negative experience. (p. 124)

Teaching the young child is a matter not just of providing opportunities to learn knowledge and skills but also of developing attitudes towards learning and using those skills. An example of how dispositions have an impact on school skills is the disposition to read. How a child feels about reading and whether or not the child wants to learn to read can have long-range effects on the child's reading achievement. We know that skills involved in reading improve by actually reading. Thus the disposition to be a "reader" must be strengthened and monitored (Katz, 1995). The National Association for the Education of Young Children specified in the guidelines for constructing appropriate curriculum that "curriculum promotes the development of knowledge and understanding, processes, and skills, as well as the dispositions to use and apply skills and to go on learning" (Bredekamp & Copple, 1997, p. 20).

The literature applying recent research on brain development and thinking to education has also had an impact on early childhood teachers' commitment to active, engaging methods that foster positive dispositions (Hart, 1983; Howard, 1994; Jensen, 1996; Sylwester, 1995). One insight from brain research is that learning is related to children's feelings and emotions, thus potentially influencing the important dispositions to learning (Howard, 1994). Not only are children less likely to practice and perfect skills if they are not positively involved, but children's feelings about an experience also affect how successful the child is in learning the skill in the first place (Sylwester, 1995).

A second insight from brain research is that learning is easier when experiences are interconnected rather than isolated or compartmentalized into subject areas (Howard, 1994). From brain research also comes the understanding that the brain adapts and develops through continuously changing and challenging environments (Kotulak, 1993). Children, especially in the early years of schooling, learn from hands-on, thought-provoking experiences because these experiences challenge children to think. According to Frank Smith (1990):

> Teachers should demonstrate the power and possibilities of thought in everything they do, and by never engaging their students in meaningless,

thoughtless activity. Students should be empowered to explore the power and possibilities of thought themselves, by seeing others explore, examine, question, and argue, and by being permitted to behave similarly. (p. 125)

In addition, experience in the early years builds a foundation for symbolic and abstract thinking. "In the first years of life, young children ... develop at least a first-draft level of competence with basic human symbol systems—language, number, music, two-dimensional depiction, and the like" (Gardner, 1993, p. 56)

Despite the prominence of recommendations for active, engaging, and meaningful learning experiences and the literature on brain development, teaching young children in ways that they learn best is not always supported by decision makers and parents. Educators have felt increasing challenges created by social and economic changes. When it appeared that children were having difficulty learning, some staff in some schools became anxious and mistakenly transferred methods that are not appropriate from the elementary years into the early years. This was based on a belief that beginning academic instruction earlier would result in higher achievement. Many early childhood programs placed undue emphasis on rote learning and whole-group instruction of narrowly defined academic skills (Bredekamp & Copple, 1997).

In response to this phenomenon, the National Association for the Education of Young Children issued the first position statement on developmentally appropriate practices (Bredekamp, 1987). This position statement was very influential in challenging teachers to think about what was appropriate in early childhood classrooms. In the revised version (Bredekamp & Copple, 1997), 12 principles of child development and learning were articulated (see Figure 1.1). These accurately summarize our beliefs about appropriate early childhood programming.

WHY DOCUMENT?

Through documentation the teacher can make it possible for others to "see" the learning that takes place when developmentally appropriate teaching occurs. Documentation also provides the evidence needed for reliably assessing children's progress, for meeting accountability requirements, for monitoring individual students' growth and development, and for program evaluation.

Often as teachers become more and more committed to teaching children appropriately and fostering positive dispositions, they become concerned about the use of standardized group achievement tests to assess children's development.

Figure 1.1 Principles of Child Development and Learning

1. Domains of children's development—physical, social, emotional, and cognitive—are closely related. Development in one domain influences and is influenced by development in other domains.
2. Development occurs in a relatively orderly sequence, with later abilities, skills, and knowledge building on those already acquired.
3. Development proceeds at varying rates from child to child as well as unevenly within different areas of each child's functioning.
4. Early experiences have both cumulative and delayed effects on individual children's development; optimal periods exist for certain types of development and learning.
5. Development proceeds in predictable directions toward greater complexity, organization and internalization.
6. Development and learning occur in and are influenced by multiple social and cultural contexts.
7. Children are active learners, drawing on direct physical and social experiences as well as culturally transmitted knowledge to construct their own understandings of the world around them.
8. Development and learning result from interaction of biological maturation and the environment, which includes both the physical and social worlds that children live in.
9. Play is an important vehicle for children's social, emotional, and cognitive development as well as a reflection of their development.
10. Development advances when children have opportunities to practice newly acquired skills as well as when they experience a challenge just beyond the level of their present mastery.
11. Children demonstrate different modes of knowing and learning and different ways of representing what they know.
12. Children develop and learn best in the context of a community where they are safe and valued, their physical needs are met and they feel psychologically secure.

Source: Bredekamp & Copple (1996), *Developmentally Appropriate Practices,* Rev. Ed., pp. 10–15

Meeting Accountability Demands

An important impetus for documentation is accountability. Funding of early childhood programs is under scrutiny, along with all other government expenditures. In light of severe competition for scarce public funds, providing evidence of program effectiveness has become essential. Results are more closely monitored than in the past with requirements to inform the constituencies of schools and other early childhood programs of their effectiveness. As programs attempted to meet demands for accountability, some of them turned to increased use of standardized tests.

However, group-administered tests are inappropriate for assessing young children. According to Samuel Meisels (1993), group-administered tests focus on the acquisition of simple facts, low-level skills, superficial memorization, and isolated evidence of achievement. Their content is generally abstract, verbally mediated, and potentially biased against children unfamiliar or uncomfortable with testlike activities and with middle-class manners and mores. Many educators have expressed special concern about the use of standardized achievement tests with young children, and the Association for Childhood Education has issued a position statement on the topic (Perrone, 1991). Gullo (1994) explains why young children are especially affected:

> During most of the early childhood years, it is difficult to measure and assess bits of knowledge and skills that are isolated from other types of knowledge and skills. Young children are not reliable test takers due to the many different confining personal, developmental, and environmental factors that affect their behaviors. In addition, just as children do not develop in an isolated manner, they do not acquire knowledge nor learn specific bits of information or skills without learning other things within the contextual framework. (p. 15)

Gullo also raises the issue of the importance of the context of learning and using knowledge and skills. Standardized achievement tests, with their narrow focus, do not provide information about how children integrate their learning and apply content knowledge to real-life challenges. An example of this is the child who can score well on spelling lists of memorized words but misspells those same words when they are used in writing a story or a letter. Problem solving, which involves knowing what skills to apply when, is also not easily assessed by conventional methods. There is a need to assess the child's ability to integrate and apply what is learned in the more formal parts of the curriculum, such as school skills like spelling, to less formal parts of the curriculum, such as project work.

All of the concerns about standardized testing for the preprimary- and primary-age child provide additional impetus for learning to document. Teachers are being challenged to apply developmentally appropriate curriculum and teaching methods and, at the same time, to provide evidence of growth, development, and intellectual and social learning. The two circles in Figure 1.2 represent these two simultaneous challenges. Teachers want to meet demands of accountability placed upon them. They also want to know how to use informal methods for assessment and program evaluation that would show what children are learning and give credibility to the teaching and learning processes occurring in their classrooms. Figure 1.2 also shows how comprehensive, careful, systematic documentation of the learning that occurs when children are involved in meaningful learning experiences can meet the demands for both effective teaching and accountability.

Becoming Better Teachers

One of the most important reasons to learn about documentation is its power to inform teaching. "Documentation provides a basis for the modification and adjustment of teaching strategies, and a source of ideas for new strategies, while deepening teachers' awareness of each child's progress" (Katz & Chard, p. 2, 1996). It can build teachers' skills. Teachers who have good documentation skills are more likely to make productive decisions when planning educational experiences, interacting with the child and family, and accessing support systems for children. These decisions include how to organize the classroom, what to do next, what questions to ask children, what resources to provide, and how to stimulate the development of each child. The more information the teacher can gather informing these decisions, the more effective the teacher is likely to be.

Figure 1.2 Simultaneous Challenges

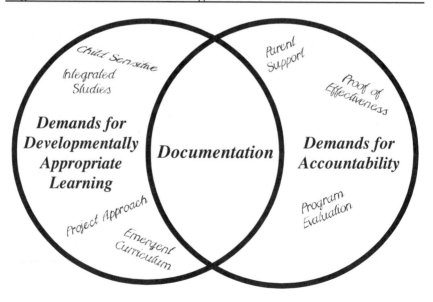

Typical assessment of children's learning using standardized tests provides limited assistance in teacher decision making. Vygotsky's socio-cultural theory of maximizing learning demonstrates the most serious insufficiency of traditional methods of assessment and of monitoring children's development (Berk & Winsler, 1995; Bodrova & Leong, 1996; Vygotsky, 1978). "Vygotsky suggested that what we should be measuring is not what children can do by themselves or already know but rather what they can do with help or another person and have the potential to learn" (Berk & Winsler, 1995, p. 26). According to Vygotsky, the teacher is most effective when teaching is directed toward a *zone of proximal development* for each child. Vygotsky presents learning as a continuum (see Figure 1.3). The *actual developmental level* is what the student has already mastered. The *zone of proximal development* is what the student is beginning to understand, what the student can do sometimes and not other times, and what the student can do with help. This is where progress in learning is maximized. The *potential developmental level* is new knowledge or skills that the child has not yet achieved. The student moves through this continuum as new knowledge is integrated with old knowledge and new skills are mastered. The zone of proximal development is dynamic and changing constantly as children acquire new skills and knowledge. As Bodrova and Leong (1996) explain:

> Vygotsky chose the word *zone* because he conceived development not as a point on a scale, but as a continuum of behaviors or degrees of maturation. By describing the zone as proximal (next to, close to), he meant that the zone is limited by those behaviors that will develop in the *near* future. (p. 35)

Figure 1.3 Vygotsky's Zone of Proximal Development

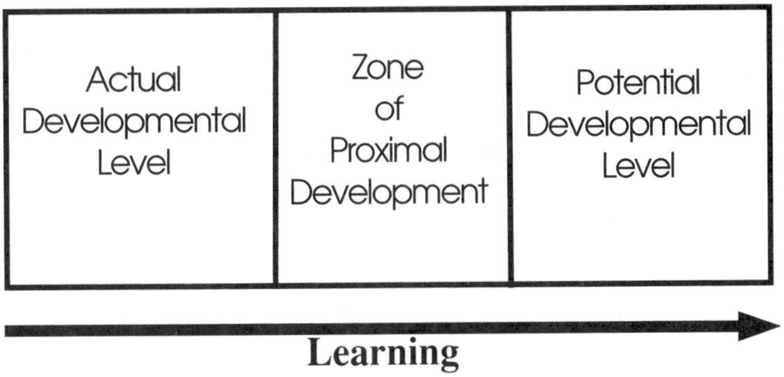

According to Berk & Winsler (1995), a major goal of education is to keep children working in the zone of proximal development. The teacher can do that by structuring the task and the environment and adjusting the amount of adult intervention to the child's current needs and abilities. To do this requires that teachers have in-depth and current understanding about the knowledge and skills of their students. This has great implications for assessment practices. To determine the zone, a teacher needs to assess a child's development, probe the child's thinking on the topic, and provide learning experiences that will build a bridge or scaffold to higher-level thought processes or *potential learning*. To do this successfully, it is important that the teacher know not only what a child can already do independently but also what the child can do with different levels of assistance. Teachers also need to know how children use their help and what hints are most useful (Bodrova & Leong, 1996).

Standardized tests do not assist the teacher in teaching to the zone of development. They focus on a limited sample of what the student has mastered. By using only information on what children already know, the teacher cannot as effectively assist the child in reaching the next stages of learning. In addition, the time delay between administration of standardized group tests and availability of results to teachers precludes using this data to inform teachers of the zone of proximal development.

Meeting Diversity Challenges

Teachers are also interested in documentation because of the demographic changes in classrooms. In many communities, children are coming to preschool with unmet needs and the role of the teacher has become more complex. Changing demographics have increased the skills required for an early childhood teacher to be effective. Teachers are finding more and more children in their classrooms who are growing up in poverty, and the challenge of successfully supporting their growth and development is greater (Children's Defense Fund, 1995). Because mothers are returning to the work force early in their child's life, even children from families with adequate income are spending a significant amount of their growth and learning time under the direction of early childhood teachers in group settings (Children's Defense Fund, 1995). With the increase in single-parent families and the increasing economic challenge to support young families, many parents have little time and energy to participate in schools and interact daily with their children. Today's teacher, in addition to being responsible for effective teaching in the classroom, often takes more responsibility for assisting parents in understanding and supporting their children's learning.

Inclusion of children with special needs in regular education class-rooms has also increased the complexity of teaching. These include children who are gifted, have physical disabilities, have learning problems requiring individualized education plans, speak English as a second language, and have problems resulting from growing up in poverty. Teachers need to know what children do and do not know, as well as how they learn most easily so that methods can be adjusted to help them learn in the most effective way—teachers do not want to waste children's time and effort. It is also important to be sure that information teachers are using for decision making is unbiased and culturally sensitive. Documentation can help the teacher identify and provide the appropriate learning experiences for all children as well as more typically developing children.

Changes in typical approaches to meeting diverse needs are also common. Some of these changes have resulted in a greater need for documentation. For example, there are new approaches to meeting the needs of children in classrooms with a high percentage of children in poverty. In the past, teachers in such classrooms often focused on what children lacked with intensive drill and practice on discrete skills. Teachers moved children as a group through a fixed sequence of subskills, and assessment was through standardized tests. Several decades of studies of successful teaching in such classrooms now point to the value of de-emphasizing the teaching of discrete skills in isolation from the context in which these skills are applied, fostering connections between academic learning and the world from which children come, and using the child and the child's experiences as a resource for learning (Knapp, 1995). The emphasis is now on strategies that provide extensive opportunities for engaging children in activities that require reading, writing, and problem-solving skills.

In contrast to standardized achievement or subskill testing, which does not provide information teachers need, comprehensive, quality documentation can assist teachers in teaching children from high poverty backgrounds. Similarly, documentation can assist teachers in meeting special needs of other children through productive, efficient, and developmentally matched teaching methods.

Involving Children and Families

Watching children learn is exciting and rewarding to teachers. They understand the importance of developing a culture of a learning school where children see themselves as learners, parents see their children as successful learners and members of the community value the learning that occurs. Early childhood teachers need to know how to develop documentation systems that are planned to involve children and families as participants as well as viewers. Teachers need to use a variety of ways to document so they can show all of the children's strengths and unique talents. They need to know how to collect and present evidence of children's learning so that people with a wide range of backgrounds and interests can understand the meaning of the documentation.

Teachers also want documentation to assist in developing partnerships with parents. A carefully planned and implemented documentation process can assist teachers in informing and reassuring parents. For example, a parent might express concern that his child is not writing real words at the beginning of kindergarten. A teacher who has collected samples of children's writing may be able to ease these fears by showing the child's progress through the child's writing samples that she has collected. Through examining the samples and hearing what the teacher has to say about typical progress, the parent can see that children progress from letterlike shapes, to clear letters, to words. The parent can then appreciate how his child is progressing through the normal sequence and can share with the teacher what he has observed at home. The parent, whose anxieties are eased, will not endanger the child's disposition to write by placing undue pressure on the child, such as extensive drill and practice of making "correct" letters at home. Together the teacher and parent can develop ideas to use at home that will show the child how important writing and reading are in the home. The parent can put his efforts into providing a literacy-enriched environment, and the teacher can share her documentation of the child's ongoing progress toward literacy.

Documentation can also assist parents in making decisions about their child's education. In the following note a parent, Nancy Higgins, explains how she came to understand the project approach through a documentation display and how it assisted her in choosing a preschool program for her child.

> My first actual encounter with projects occurred in late spring at an open house for prospective parents. Because my husband was out of town, I had to attend alone. I tried to analyze the project approach in the manner he might have. I was skeptical—the so-called traditional approaches had worked for me, so why wouldn't it also provide success for our child. . . . Walking around the school that night, I began to be impressed. I studied [the documentation on] a project on reflections. I marveled at the insights shared by the children. The critical

thinking skills which their work exhibited was phenomenal. Direct quotations included sentences of greater length and complexity than I would have expected. Their vocabulary was very specific. I went home and attempted to describe what I had seen to my husband. . . . After our discussion, we became convinced that this was the place for our daughter to learn.

Having gained a clear understanding of the curriculum and teaching methods of the school, this parent felt confident about the decision to enroll her child.

Documentation can also assist the teacher in making decisions about when additional support systems are needed for a child. As a teacher becomes a skilled documenter, she can improve her knowledge and understanding of the typical development of children's knowledge and skills. When collecting a child's work over a period of time, she can see if a child is progressing as expected and if mastery of a skill is just around the corner. When the teacher does not see mastery or emerging skills, she can seek additional help and special assistance can be provided for the child.

Providing a Vehicle for Reflection

Documentation reveals to us not only what children are learning but also what teachers are learning about teaching. Documentation can be a vehicle for self-reflection and a way to analyze, share, discuss, and guide the process of teaching by communicating with other professionals what is occurring in the classroom. Teachers teach by making dozens of decisions each day. Bredekamp & Copple (1997) recognize the importance of these decisions when they define "developmentally appropriate practice as the outcome of decision making" (p. vii). Teachers are challenged from a variety of sources to become more reflective, to regularly analyze, evaluate, and strengthen the quality and effectiveness of their work (National Board for Professional Teaching Standards, 1996). To do this, they need to accurately capture what is occurring in the classroom through documentation.

THE PROMISE OF DOCUMENTATION

Learning to document yields positive results when a teacher makes a commitment of time and effort. Teaching in developmentally appropriate ways is facilitated when teachers know how to obtain and provide evidence of children's learning that occurs when teachers use developmentally appropriate teaching methods (Bredekamp, 1987). In contrast to standardized achievement tests, comprehensive, good-quality documentation can do the following:

- Provide evidence of children's learning in all areas of a child's development: physical, emotional, social, and cognitive
- Offer insight into the complex learning experiences provided to children when teachers use an integrated approach
- Provide a framework for organizing teachers' observations and recording each child's special interests and developmental progress
- Emphasize learning as an interactive process by documenting what children learn when they are engaged in active exploration and interaction with adults, other children, and materials
- Show the advantages of activities and materials that are concrete, real, and relevant to the lives of young children
- Enable the teacher to assess what children know or can and cannot do so the teacher can modify the difficulty, complexity, and challenge of an activity as children are involved with it and as they develop understanding and skills

When teachers document children's learning in a variety of ways, they can be more confident about the value of their teaching.

CHAPTER 2

Windows on Learning:
A Framework for Decision Making

window: —1. An opening constructed in a wall or roof to admit light or air.
—*American Heritage Dictionary* (1994)

For documentation to yield the benefits outlined in Chapter 1, the methods used must be simple, organized, and efficient so that they enhance rather than detract from a teacher's productivity. Good-quality documentation enables the three major players in the child's educational experience—teachers, parents, and community—to respond more accurately to the true needs of the child in the education system. In this way, the education system can work more consistently with, rather than against, teachers in their efforts, thereby enhancing effectiveness. But how do teachers decide what and when to document? How extensive should the documentation be? How should the documentation be presented?

Answers to these questions depend on the use of sound theoretical frameworks for making decisions about focus, presentation, and extensiveness of documentation. Our theoretical frameworks are presented using the image of three windows. First, a *Window on a Child's Development* provides a framework for the teacher to document and share with others an individual child's growth and development. Second, a *Window on a Learning Experience* provides a framework for the teacher to document and share with others a specific learning experience of the class. Third, a *Window for Teacher Self-Reflection* provides the teacher with a framework for documenting his or her role in the learning experience. To visualize the use of these frameworks, begin with an image of a classroom where children are deeply engaged in project work. Constructions are coming together; scenes are unfolding in the dramatic play area; some children are totally absorbed in an individual activity; some children are working together, talking and planning; and teachers are interacting with children. These activities are typical of the bustle of a classroom in which children's minds are fully engaged in a variety of meaningful activities. Now imagine that three windows have been inserted into the walls of this busy classroom, to enable others to look in. They represent the three ways of looking at the learning that occurs in classrooms. Each window provides a different perspective on the learning processes, by means of which adults and children can gain insight. Selecting a window guides the teacher in choosing the particular aspect of the project to be documented, the form of documentation, and the degree of elaboration in the description.

A WINDOW ON A CHILD'S DEVELOPMENT

By providing documentation to form a window on an individual child, a teacher may share insights regarding a child's growth and development with the child's parents and/or with colleagues. The teacher may improve the accuracy of his or her own view of the child through periodic, systematic examination of individual documentation. Documentation through this window will focus on individually produced items or on evidence of the individual child's participation in the group. Individual products that constitute documentation may include items commonly collected for children's portfolios, such as examples of the child's drawing, writing, constructions, or songs. The benefits of the principle that "the more informed you are, the better able you are to make decisions" (L. G. Katz, personal communication, August 16, 1995) are applicable here.

Another type of documentation that provides a window on the child's development is the child's self-reflections, which may be collected in tape recordings, anecdotal notes, webs made by the individual child, or a child's contributions to webs made by a group. An example of a self-reflection that includes a statement of disposition or feeling was collected in the course of a project conducted in Judy Cagle's preprimary classroom for 3- and 4-year-olds:

> Taylor was one of several children using clay and small pieces of mylar to construct small buildings. Taylor is a very verbal child with strong language skills, but he had shown a marked lack of interest in using art materials. However, the Reflections Project really engaged Taylor's interest, and he constructed an elaborate clay church with many entrances and windows. He painted the clay structure orange and cut and carefully glued mylar windows onto his church. Completing his church took Taylor several days. On completion of his construction, Taylor turned to me and said, "Teacher, this is the best

thing I've ever done in my whole life!" I thought this statement was especially significant in view of Taylor's earlier avoidance of the art materials.

That day Ms. Cagle noted in her journal Taylor's self-appraisal and newfound satisfaction with his art ability. She made a note to herself to build on Taylor's interest in representing buildings in three dimensions by presenting him with alternative materials for construction. Later that week she recorded the statement as an anecdotal record in Taylor's portfolio and recorded his self-appraisal on his developmental checklist (Dichtelmiller, Jablon, Dorfman, Marsden, & Meisels, 1994). Since she considered this statement to be such a milestone in his development, Ms. Cagle displayed a photograph of Taylor's church in the hallway.

She wanted Taylor's parents to see the construction he had built in the art area and to recognize that his statement indicated a new positive evaluation of himself as an artist. The item on the developmental check-list that Ms. Cagle supported with her documentation of Taylor's state-ment was VI A-1 in "The Arts" section of the Work Sampling System: "Uses a variety of art materials for tactile experience and explo-ration"(Jablon, Marsden, Meisels, & Dichtelmiller, 1994, p. 162).

As shown in the example, observations of a child's development made during the course of a project may take the form of data points on a developmental checklist, or of anecdotal notes or statements on disposi-tions. Items of work saved for a child's individual portfolio might include photos, tape recordings, and samples or products.

As in the case of Taylor, the teacher selects those items for documen-tation that indicate significant growth or development and displays those items that reveal growth and that may, at the same time, tell the story of the project. Had Ms. Cagle attempted to document for display the comments of all the children in her class who had chosen to construct buildings with clay, she would have needlessly used time and space and consequently reduced her own efficiency. In addition, had she uniformly displayed all the children's comments, those viewing the display might have overlooked the importance of Taylor's statement. A teacher who documents effectively looks for and displays work that provides evi-dence of each child's growth and development.

On occasion a teacher might create a minidisplay that focuses on the growth of a child who has been particularly engaged in a project. This minidisplay, then, might be included in the larger display documenting the development of the project. More typically, however, the teacher publicly documents a project using the work of many children in the class. In this way, all children have work displayed, but not all children have *all* their work displayed at the same time. For example, part of a display of a Rabbit Project might be made up of a writing sample from one child, a drawing sample from another child, and a tape-recorded sample of a song about rabbits created by another. Each sample is selected because of the growth it reveals in the individual child's development, but in their totality, the various samples also tell the story of the project.

A WINDOW ON A LEARNING EXPERIENCE

When the purpose of the documentation is to organize, demonstrate, and display to others the general growth in knowledge, skills, dispositions, and feelings (Chard, 1994) of the children involved in a learning experience, the teacher may select documentation to form another window. The view through this window enables the teacher to share the impact of the project on the children's learning with other teachers, parents, or visitors.

Items for documentation might be such group products as songs, writing, constructions, webs, drawings, or paintings. These are often accompanied by narratives written by the teacher, the children, or both together. An excellent example of the creation of a Window on a Learning Experience is present in Mary Ann Gottlieb's narrative of the mini-project that her multi-age class, ages 5 and 6, experienced as part of their Water Project. This narrative, along with photographs and samples of the children's work included in a display, made it possible for others to see into the learning experience.

> When we first webbed the topic *water*, the children thought of many ways we use water at home. Candy suggested we make a house showing how water gets into the house where we use it, and then how water leaves the house. We investigated different kinds of houses, creating and drawing various kinds of homes. Danny was an expert on trailers, since he lived in one. He said, "My house doesn't have a basement or upstairs. But we have a yard and a place to play."
>
> We decided to construct a single-family home and studied Mrs. Beneke's dollhouse for additional information. After drawing that house, we made a list of materials we needed for construction. We measured the dollhouse and began collecting paper boxes. Charles said that taping the boxes together would be "ugly." Michael suggested that we "hot glue" the boxes together and offered to bring his

mother's glue gun. Ms. Gottlieb glued the boxes, but they did not remain stable. Finally we tried brads and were satisfied with the results.

Janay traced the roof of the dollhouse onto the cardboard, did the cutting, assisted in mixing the paint ("You need to add more white . . . more . . . OK.") so that it matched the dollhouse, and painted the roof.

We collected paper towel tubes to use for the pipes. However, once they were assembled into lengths, the tubes proved to be too large for indoor piping. Another discussion resulted in Demetrus suggesting that we use pencils. "I'll tape them together along the edge," he said. He used his scissors to score and then cut them into proper sizes. Bigger pencils were used for the waste-water pipes. By using different colored pencils, Michael said that "you can tell which pipes have clean water and which pipes carry dirty water." He was careful to place the plumbing fixtures in places where the pipes ran.

After seeing and representing a real water meter, Carl made a water meter for outside the house. His knowledge of how meters look enabled him to select appropriate materials and work independently.

Furniture was made with "found items." Many children participated in its construction. Stephen and Charles worked together to build the bedroom furniture. Tiara and Andrea made the washer and dryer. Michael and Justin H. tried several materials before finally constructing the bathtub.

The house is not finished. Justin H. plans to make drain pipes leading away from the house. The pictures, mirrors, and most of the curtains are yet to be constructed and hung. The appliances and plumbing fixtures are complete.

Panels of mounted documentation, books for parents, notes of teacher discussions with other staff, teacher journals and project journals are useful types of documentation for this view of the learning experience.

Documenting to provide a Window on a Learning Experience using a narrative of the project also enables the teachers to model a useful process for children. They can explain their purpose in selecting items for documentation and the ways they choose to display and write about them. They can solicit the children's ideas about what should be included in the narrative of the project. The children can then incorporate this knowledge of the process in creating their own documentation of their individual and group projects to share with other children and adults, thereby deepening their understanding of the project, their place within it, and the relationship of the project to those outside the classroom who will read the documentation. Creating their own documentation helps children to "construct an identity and find a place within . . . [their] culture" (Bruner, 1996, p. 42). The desire for such a transfer of the documentation process from adult to child is apparent in a summary of project documentation by Gail Gordon, a preprimary teacher:

> Documentation of our project activities is displayed in the hallway for parents, teachers, administrators, and the community to view. The history of the project, displayed with a summary sheet, photos, comments, and work samples will be on display for a while to encourage the children to review and reflect upon their learning. The photos, constructions, and artwork serve as a boost to the children's memory, enabling them to revisit the activities. I am hoping that they will be able to use these representations to report the activities to others. Reporting to other students, parents, and visitors will help them deepen their understanding of the project topic and demonstrate their communication skills and enthusiasm for project work.

By demonstrating the process of selecting information for the project narrative, by writing documentation to explain the significance of the items she selects to accompany the project narrative, and by considering the potential of the items she selects to boost the children's memories, Ms. Gordon has created a Window on a Learning Experience. This documentation enables her, as a teacher, to understand a specific learning experience of her students. Furthermore, the documentation can be shared with others. She has also modeled a process for children to emulate.

A WINDOW FOR TEACHER SELF-REFLECTION

A teacher may create this third type of window, a Window for Teacher Self-Reflection, when her purpose is to reflect on her role in the learning experience of the children up until that point in time and to evaluate and revise her role based on that reflection. She may use documentation such as entries in her daily journal, observations and suggestions from colleagues, and feedback from parents and the children themselves to evaluate her effectiveness in guiding the children through a project. She may revisit a web in which she has "forecasted" (S. C. Chard, personal communication, August 15, 1995) project activities as part of her planning process and compared the activities on the web with the type and quantity of activities that were actually generated by the project. She may also assess the amount of involvement by the individual children in the class as recorded and dated on the web.

The documentation the teacher brings together for this purpose allows him to reflect on and improve the quality of his own judgment of the development of the individual children in his class and the class as a whole as they engage in project work. The more accurately a teacher can "read" a child's knowledge, skills, dispositions, and feelings (S. C. Chard, personal communication, August 15, 1995), the better able he is both to gauge the child's zone of proximal development and to provoke growth in the child by tapping the child's intrinsic motivation. Once the teacher has an accurate picture of each individual in his class, he is better able to assess the effectiveness of his teaching to the group and the individual child. The essence of good teaching is judgment based on good information. Good information for teaching the class as a whole comes from the teacher's reflections over time on the individual children in his class as they engage in learning experiences. Reflecting on his teaching enables him to make decisions, such as what materials to provide and what situations to set up to simultaneously engage all children in learning. In a sense, he judges the zone of proximal development of the group as a whole.

As she begins a project with the children, a teacher can anticipate the need for documentation for each aspect of the project. As the project develops, the teacher may refer back to this documentation to monitor the need for changes in methods. Gail Gordon's self-reflection as entered in her teacher journal on the Baby Project is a case in point:

> Project teaching is as engaging for the teachers as for the students, and as it emerges it becomes necessary to make decisions about selecting materials, evaluating progress, and timing learning experiences. Our project is still in process. Some children may be interested in constructing a baby swing for our baby area. We are going to decide together to extend or to culminate activities. I look forward to children reporting their learning to parents and friends.

And, finally, as the project is completed, this window allows the teacher to gain insight by which to improve the effectiveness of her methods and to plan for further professional development. As she continues in her journal, Ms. Gordon reflects on the experience she and her assistant have had as part of the project.

We are growing in our abilities to slow down and listen to the interests and developmental needs of the children. We are learning to be more flexible in lesson planning and more willing to schedule large blocks of uninterrupted time. We are learning to create space in the classroom for project materials and children's work-in-process. Children and teachers are valuing work more by keeping it at school to continue and refine. We understand more fully the importance of allowing children to work out solutions to problems they may encounter. We realize that we need to revisit topics to study them in more depth.

Over time, documentation for self-reflection provides the vehicle for the teacher to improve the accuracy and efficiency of the documentation she provides for the Window on a Child's Development and the Window on a Learning Experience. Consequently, the view through the Window for Teacher Self-Reflection has perhaps the greatest potential impact of the three.

CHAPTER 3

The Documentation Web: Providing a Map for Documentation

web 5: —A complex, interconnected structure or arrangement.
—*American Heritage Dictionary* (1994)

"The world can doubtless never be well known by theory: practice is absolutely necessary; but surely it is of great use to a young man, before he sets out for that country, full of mazes, windings, and turnings, to have at least a general map of it, made by some experienced traveler."
—Lord Chesterfield (1694–1773). Letter, August 30, 1749

HISTORY OF THE WEB

Most teachers have some familiarity with documenting children's learning. They may use a developmental checklist required in a specific educational program, or they may use anecdotal notes to provide information for parents. They may systematically collect some children's work, such as self-portraits at the beginning and the end of the year. Teachers may not, however, be fully aware of how many options are available for assessing and demonstrating children's learning. The teachers described in this book have been focusing on developing their skill as documenters. As several of these teachers also became more involved with the project approach, the study of the process of documentation in projects became a focus of professional development.

Webbing

It is sometimes helpful when learning a new skill or new content knowledge to explore a variety of ways of thinking about the topic. Radiant thinking, and the expression of that thinking as a mind map (Buzan & Buzan, 1996), is a graphic technique that focuses the thinker on a central image. The main themes of the subject radiate from the central image like branches. A similar technique, called webbing, is also a common method of studying projects. Webbing is a way to determine children's knowledge before they begin a study and to follow the progress of the growth of that knowledge throughout a project.

Sylvia Chard (1994) describes the process of developing a web:

> The process of making a topic web enables the teacher to use his or her own general knowledge of the topic as a starting point for planning the project. Each individual person has very similar but slightly differently organized mind maps of any given topic. When the teacher starts with her own mind map or web she becomes more interested in the topic and curious about her own knowledge. She can also more easily evaluate the ideas which children offer and incorporate them appropriately into the planning. (p. 33)

As teachers documented children's learning using topic webs and we became acquainted with the concept of mind mapping, we naturally began to document our own learning about the process of documentation by drawing a web. The first web of types of documentation was developed by Helm and Beneke for the staff of the Valeska Hinton Early Childhood Education Center. The purpose was to assist teachers in expanding their concepts of how they might collect evidence of children's learning and to support their developing skills in documentation. This web then became a map for discussion and experimentation by the teachers at the Center and at other schools.

Nessa and the Point of View

As the web was shared with other schools, an additional staff development activity was designed to accompany the introduction of the web. This activity was inspired by an experience viewing photographs of a chair from different angles at the Reggio Institute. In the staff development activity that accompanied training on the web, a large bag was placed on a table in the center of the room. In the bag was a small wooden chair with a high back. On the chair was a doll named Nessa. Teachers sat in a large circle around the edge of the room. As the bag was pulled off, revealing Nessa and the chair, everyone drew a picture of exactly what they saw. After everyone completed their drawings, members of the group walked around the room and viewed each other's drawings and compared them.

The variations were extensive. Sketches varied depending on where the artist was sitting in the room. Some pictures showed only the back of the chair and no doll. Some showed the side of the chair with just the tip of Nessa's hand showing. Some showed all of Nessa. These variations were caused by the position, or viewing point, of each artist. Even more revealing were the other variations. Some drawings were very large and some very small. Some had extensive detail and some were mere sketches. Some artists drew Nessa and the chair and a few drew only Nessa. Some artists drew Nessa, the chair, the table, or even the other artists drawing Nessa. After this experience with a change in point of view, a discussion followed about the similarities between the drawing experience and how different people view the child and his or her experience in school. Variations were again discussed, but this time regarding differences in the perception of learning, school, the role of the teacher, and so forth. This experience focused the teachers on the need to consider other viewpoints, to expect variations in how different people would interpret information about a child, how they would bring to the experience their own point of view. Teachers began to realize that parents, children, colleagues, administrators, and members of the community at large might be looking at the learning that occurred in their classrooms in very different ways. Even though the teacher may plan documentation to provide a specific window or view of a child or learning experience, the viewer's point of view limits and expands what is seen. A clear vision of the need for a variety of ways to provide evidence of learning and the need to communicate that evidence emerged. Documentation of children's work began to fill the hallways of their schools.

UNDERSTANDING THE DOCUMENTATION WEB

The web grew and changed as teachers shared their projects, the ways in which they collected and communicated about the learning that occurred, and as they developed ways to present documentation with different points of view. The web shown in Figure 3.1 groups the variety of ways of gathering evidence about children's learning around the central topic of types of documentation. Radiating out from the web are five clusters: individual portfolios, project narratives, observations of child development, products (individual or group), and child self-reflections. Each of these types of documentation can provide a way to view children's work.

The web is not an exhaustive list of all possible types of documentation. There are as many different ways to document learning as there are

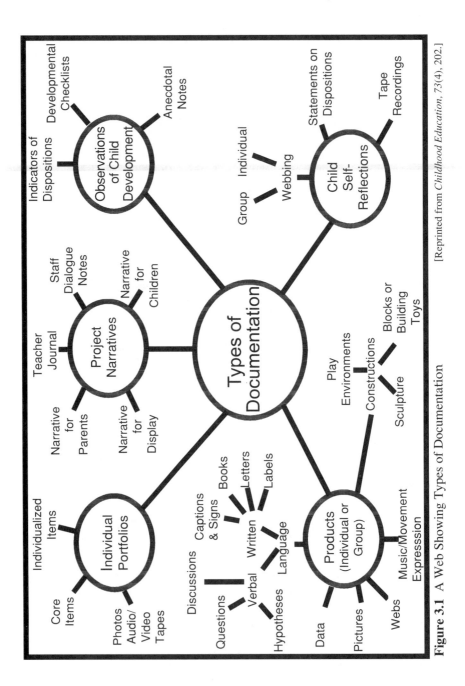

[Reprinted from *Childhood Education, 73*(4), 202.]

Figure 3.1 A Web Showing Types of Documentation

ways that active, engaged children try to make sense of their world. The web is also not meant to be an exclusive classification system for evidence of children's learning. Just as a teacher can design a specific learning experience that will stimulate a variety of areas of a child's development, one sample of a child's work may be considered as more than one type of documentation. For example, an anecdotal note about a child's first attempt to write a word on a drawing about a project could become part of an individual portfolio or it could become part of a project history book that provides a narrative about the project. The web stimulates discussion about documentation by providing a vocabulary and a structure for teachers to communicate with one another about documentation and decision making.

USING THE WEB TO INCREASE VARIATION

The documentation web can remind teachers of the variety of ways to document. Documentation is most effective when teachers vary their documentation to match the learning experiences of the children and to meet the needs of the audiences for whom the documentation is intended. The more familiar a teacher becomes with the variety of types of documentation, the more options the teacher has to select the most appropriate one. For example, a teacher who wanted to know what a child knew about a project topic might think about collecting the child's drawings and written work about the project. After reviewing the types of documentation, the teacher might also decide to have the child participate in constructing a new revised web about what he or she knows about the topic, or have the child dictate a narrative to accompany a photographic display about the project. Using a variety of ways to document also helps the teacher to get accurate information from a particular child. For example, a child who has not devloped extensive language skills may not be able to dictate a narrative but may be able to draw a picture or construct a block play environment that reveals the depth of understanding the child has about the topic.

This approach of gathering a variety of kinds of evidence of children's learning and thinking is also more compatible with today's understanding of and emphasis on the variability in how people think and learn. Howard Gardner's (1983) theory of multiple intelligences has helped teachers to recognize that there are more valid ways of learning than the traditional school focus on the development of verbal/language and logical/mathematical thinking. Attention should also be paid to children's musical, visual/spatial, body/kinesthetic, interpersonal, and intrapersonal intelligences. Traditional ways of measuring learning often do not enable the teacher to look at these other intelligences.

Each cluster on the web is discussed separately in Chapters 4 through 8 of this book. Each individual chapter focuses on how that type of documentation looks in real classrooms and the ways a teacher can use that type of documentation. Samples of documentation from projects and other classroom activities show how the specific type of documentation can be integrated with teaching and how teachers can use it to determine teaching strategies.

CHAPTER 4

Project Narratives: Telling the Story

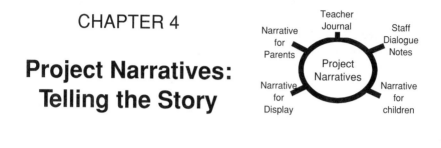

narrate: —*tr.* To tell (a story, for example) in speech or writing.
—*intr.* To give an account of events.

—*American Heritage Dictionary* (1994)

Narratives that tell the story of a learning experience such as a project can be used to provide documentation for all three windows: the Window on a Child's Development, the Window on a Learning Experience, and the Window on Teacher Self-Reflection. They can take the form of stories for and by children, records of conversations with other teachers, teacher journals, narratives for parents in the form of books and letters, or visual displays.

THE STORY

Stories are a powerful way to help others understand an event or an experience that a person has had. Many learning experiences, especially projects, are, by their nature, good stories. As Sylvia Chard (1994) states, "In a sense, like a good story, the project can be described as having a beginning, a middle and an end, each memorable in its own way" (p. 40). The telling of this story by the teachers or children can provide powerful evidence of the development of skills and knowledge. An example of a narrative is the teacher journal notes of Anna Brown that were used as a narrative of the Reflections Project displayed in the hallway.

MARCH 7: Again, I asked the children to tell me what they knew about reflections and our second attempt at webbing turned into a brainstorming session from which a couple of jobs were generated. [For example, Katie suggested:] "Make a rainbow in a mirror."

MARCH 8: Katie started to work on their project. She held a prism and a flashlight before the mirror. There was no rainbow, and so she elicited the support of her classmates in gathering together our collection of small flashlights. They simultaneously shined them into the mirror. Her logic was that if you shined the lights encased in an assortment of rainbow colors on a mirror, the color of the flashlights' plastic casings would somehow become infused with the light and cast a spectrum of colors onto the mirror.

MARCH 9: Katie and Jequila worked on her project. First, they tried the flashlight and a prism; and when that did not yield the effects that they were after, Katie decided to exchange the prism for a quart of water. There was a small rainbow in the mirror; however, this did not satisfy them. Jequila collected an assortment of colored blocks and colored links. They experimented [with] placing them over the water and with lining them up in front of the mirror.

Andrew made a rainbow (drawing) and gave it to Katie to use in her project. They held the rainbow in front of the mirror, and there was a reflection of a rainbow in the mirror. Although it was not expressed, Katie seemed to be persisting in the belief that she needed the water and the light to generate a rainbow. For the next few minutes, Katie and Jequila experimented with shining the light behind Andrew's picture and with holding it over the quart of water, shining the light over and under it.

MARCH 10: Katie's mother and I talked about her project, and from Linda I learned that Katie had been discussing her plans over dinner. She was also tuning into a science show on PBS for ideas.

This story about Katie's attempt to make a rainbow in a mirror provided insight for the teacher and the parent into Katie's knowledge, skills, and dispositions (Window on a Child's Devleopment). Ms. Brown was able to determine that Katie had some knowledge about light and rainbows and the relationship of water and glass to the making of rainbows. She was able to use this information to determine what materials and experiences she should introduce into the classroom to advance Katie's knowledge. The teacher and parent both noted that Katie had developed a number of problem-solving skills. For example, she knew how to do an experiment, how to get others to think about her problem and offer solutions, and where to find helpful information. Both the teacher and the parent also noted that the story revealed Katie's curiosity and her disposition to learn. The narrative provided evidence for Ms. Brown to confidently mark Katie "proficient" on the Work Sampling developmental checklist item, "Seeks answers to questions through active exploration," in the "Scientific Thinking" domain (Jablon et al., 1994, p.124).

Later in the journal, the teacher reflected on this narrative and what she had learned about how children learn.

> The children were engaged in the project on a variety of levels. They asked questions, made observations, experimented, cooperated, and shared. . . . Their work reflects an insightfulness and persistence that I had not seen before in some of our children. . . . If I had it to do all over again, I would listen more, ask more questions, and encourage the children to experiment more. I would relax more and remember that there's nothing more important than my time with the children. There's a groove of understanding that the thoughts of children flow through; I would try to find a way of moving in that groove more often than I do.

Anna Brown later shared her insights with her colleagues during a discussion of the progress of the Reflections Project.

Children enjoy telling the story of their projects. The narratives that children produce take on many forms, such as dictated stories, pictures that show the progress of the project, and even complete books. For some children, preparing their own narrative of the project is the way that they end the story. Ten days after Katie conducted her experiments, she felt motivated to finish her part of the Reflections Project by recording the experience in drawings and words.

> MARCH 20: I asked Katie if she's finished with getting a rainbow to reflect into a mirror. She tells me that she is. Later, while I am working on paperwork, she indicates that she wants to work on it again. She works out a plan and shares it with me. Her plan seems to be a history of the work she did on her part of the project. [see Figure 4.1.]

COLLECTING STORIES

Narratives are a valuable way to document learning. Parts of the narrative of a project are usually written over a period of time, making change and growth in knowledge, skills, and dispositions evident. Narratives can capture the interest of a variety of audiences. Stories interest people because of their unknown endings. Another advantage of using stories to document projects is that stories help parents and other adults to understand the way that children construct their own learning through making sense and meaning of their experiences. There is an added

Figure 4.1 Katie's pictorial summary of her participation in the project

element of surprise and suspense when children are involved in active learning experiences because the outcome of the story is not highly predictable. When Beth Crider-Olcott's class began its project on the puppy Scout, she had not predicted that it would end up as an in-depth study of a veterinarian's office. When stories are shared as they are in the process of evolving, this element of surprise increases interest of adults in the project and encourages their participation and attention.

To capitalize on the evolving nature of the project, teachers sometimes write narratives to accompany hall displays and then continuously update the narrative as children's work proceeds. An example of this type of updated narrative written by teacher Renee Jackson is from the Butterfly Project. The first paragraph was the first narrative that was posted. The second paragraph was a follow-up narrative.

> Green Five is just beginning a study of butterflies. It all began with my trip to Kentucky. The butterflies were already in the fields and gardens. I told the children about seeing them and one thing led to another. We made a web and our study began.
>
> We have just received some very young caterpillars in the mail. The children are already planning how to record their growth and changes in the next few weeks. We also have children's predictions on how long it will be before they begin to change. It has been an exciting 2 weeks and there is lots more to learn. The children have shown in-depth thinking and creativity.

Children and adults are able to check back with the display to see the progress that the class has made in investigating their topic. This type of narrative is also especially helpful for parents because it enables them to discuss the project with their children.

Narratives written for and by children are also well received. Many children, like Katie, attempt to write their own narrative in pictures or words. These narratives are often bound into a book and made available for children to read and reread. Children enjoy these books telling the story of the completed projects. Teachers send home project history books containing photos and narratives that tell the story of a project in the children's own words. An example of a project narrative can be found in Part III, Our Mail Project. Narratives also appear on the walls of classrooms and in hallway displays. Photo captions are frequently used to tell the story of many projects.

At the Center, we have noticed that children learn from what other children are learning through hearing these stories and viewing the displays. Even very young children not directly involved in a project have become interested in what other children do. This can have a powerful effect on the children's disposition to learn. This interest can be seen in the following note from parent Nancy Higgins, reflecting on the experience of her 3-year-old daughter, Brigid.

> In her first nine weeks at this school, her class has completed a project on balls. In addition, she has proceeded to describe projects from other classes to us. She has talked about hats and babies, which is her personal favorite.

The Hat Project was done by children in the classroom next door, and the Babies Project had been done by her multi-age classroom the year before Brigid entered. Brigid learned about the projects through the oral storytelling of children and through displays and project books from the previous year's work.

DETERMINING CONTENT BY THE AUDIENCE

Many of the narratives given in the examples above are suitable for a variety of audiences: parents, children, and other teachers. However, as in all types of documentation, there are times when the narrative must be tailored to particular audiences. Narratives for children often focus on the storyline of the learning experience. They serve a valuable purpose by enabling the child to revisit and reprocess the experience and to see himself or herself as an investigator.

In narratives for parents, teachers may want to include more in-depth information, such as why a topic was selected, how a topic fits into an overall curriculum plan, or what decisions the teacher made in the progress of the project. A teacher may choose to point out through a narrative what a particular observation or event tells the teacher about a child's development. When documenting the Mail Project (see Part III), Kathy Steinheimer provided parents with additional information in the project history book that children take home to read. She indicated that the additional information was primarily for parents by putting it on colored pages. The parent could read the story in the book to the child and read the colored pages silently simultaneously or at another time. Additional teacher comments for parents were printed in a different type size and font. For example, in the middle of a series of pictures showing a debate between two children about how to make a mailbag, this comment for parents is inserted in bold letters.

Children need opportunities to discuss and argue. Thus, they will gain in their ability to persuade and compromise, two very important social skills.

Similarly, Sallee Beneke's project history book on the Meadow Project also had information targeted for children and for adults. Pages for adults were on the left-hand side of the book and were on paper with a pale flower background. Pages on the right-hand side were for children and were on beige paper. Parents could read the book to their child easily by focusing on the right-hand pages and come back at another time to study the left-hand pages.

At another time, a narrative may be written for a professional audience. When teachers prepared a display for other teachers about the Water Project, teacher Mary Ann Gottlieb chose to add this narrative to copies of Work Sampling developmental checklists.

We took a checklist for each age level and highlighted in yellow any of the indicators of development that we were able to observe in the Water Project. This was very informative to us because it showed us that we were providing experiences in all the developmental areas that we were monitoring and had actually stimulated growth in many of them.

Sometimes it is important for the narrative to be in the children's own words. This is especially appropriate when children are beginning to understand the function of print or are attempting to figure out the reading process by matching letters with spoken words. When children speak or write their opinion, it is respectful of the learning process to record in writing the comments or opinion exactly as the child says it instead of editing it for grammar or spelling. Stacy Berg took this dictation of 3- and 4-year-olds' thoughts on their progress in building a giant walk-in model of an aquarium as part of the Water Project.

Daniel: We been painting. We been hitting on the hammer and slammin the nails with the hammer.

Alyssa: We been making fish. We been drawing. We been hanging them with string and tape.

Romelle: We been cutting fish. We put chicken fence over the project—the wood. We tied fish on with wire string. We painted rocks and colored fish.

Alyssa: The fish look good to me 'cause they're colored.

Brittany: We made fish good.

Bryanna: We put fish in pretty good.

Romelle: The fish. We did a good job on them. Everyone got their fish in the right shape.

Alyssa: The rocks look not good 'cause they're messy.

Brittany: People didn't paint the whole sides of rocks.

Bryanna: We did not make good names on the fish when we wroted our names.

Romelle: The blue paint doesn't look good because it's starting to crackle up.

Defining the audience for whom the documentation is intended and deciding what to include in the narrative for that particular audience are two important documentation skills for teachers. It is neither possible nor desirable to write down or explain everything that happens in the course of a project. As the author Raymond Chandler (1997) says, "A good story cannot be devised; it has to be distilled" (p. 75). To *distill*, according to the *American Heritage Dictionary*, means to separate or extract the essential elements. Like a good storyteller, the teacher must define what is most important to communicate to the intended audience.

At the Valeska Hinton Early Childhood Education Center, as teachers became more skilled at documentation, wall displays began to appear in the hallways. To assist viewers in understanding what they were seeing and to provide teachers with a framework for the distilling process, a project summary form was developed (see Figure 4.2). The summary briefly tells the essential story elements of the project similar to a synopsis or a condensed version of a book.

The summary lists the classrooms involved, the names of the teachers, the ages of the children, and the time span of the project. Space is then provided for paragraphs under headings such as "Title" or "Focus of the Project," "History of the Project," "What the Children Learned," and "Plans for the Future." As the visitor described in the Introduction discovered, a project summary is prominently placed in a black frame near each project display.

Narratives, whether they are abbreviated, as on the project summary form and project history books, or presented to viewers in installments by evolving displays, can be extremely effective in capturing the development of knowledge and skills. Like the other types of documentation described in Chapters 5–8, they require the teacher to plan ahead, organize carefully, and be consistent and persistent about documenting.

However, narratives require more. Of all the types of documentation, it is the narrative that is most open to teacher creativity. Storytelling is an art form. A teacher who learns to tell stories well can open the windows and entice others in.

Figure 4.2 The Project Summary Sheet enables viewers of displays to get an overview of the project

---

Project Summary

Valeska Hinton Early Childhood Education Center

Teachers Gottlieb and Lockhart

Room B4   **Age Level 5–7 yrs.**   **Time Span March–April**

Title of Focus of the Project

Water Around the House—We investigated how water travels to and through the house. We became familiar with different ways water is used at home.

History of the Project

This project emerged naturally from an investigation of snow and ice. After webbing prior knowledge of water, the children webbed water around the house. A large house was constructed to exhibit the plumbing. Laundry facilities were investigated, resulting in another construction activity.

What Did the Children Learn

Through investigation the children have experienced floating and sinking properties, surface tension, and evaporation. Careers in water treatment and the plumbing trade have been explored. Knowledge has been constructed about the sources of water in the home, appliances using water, and how plumbing fixtures work.

Plans for the Future

This project will continue as we move into another project about water outdoors—specifically water in the creek. We will explore a creekbed, examine the wildlife and plant life, and construct our own creekbed.

CHAPTER 5

Observations of Child Development: Watching the Child

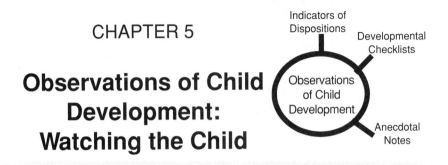

Indicators of Dispositions

Developmental Checklists

Observations of Child Development

Anecdotal Notes

observation: 1: an act or instance of observing 2: the gathering of information (as for scientific studies) by noting facts or occurrences 3: a conclusion drawn from observing.

—*Merriam-Webster Dictionary* (1994)

Observing and recording development for a variety of purposes are familiar practices for most early childhood teachers. These practices have mainly been used to report on mastery of discrete skills, to assess children's progress in school, or to indicate the frequency, duration, and nature of a behavior at a particular point in time. In general, observations of child development may be recorded as items on a developmental checklist or as anecdotal notes indicating dispositions. In recent years observation systems have been developed that expand the practical uses of the observation checklist (Cohen, 1993).

CHECKLISTS

Familiar Uses

Teachers in preschools and child-care centers often use a checklist to report on a child's mastery of school "readiness" skills. These checklists include those which are commercially produced as well as those versions produced by the teacher. Sometimes checklists are designed by a committee or group of educators who generate items based on their experience with children. They often lack validity or reliability data. These checklists are sometimes sent home with a child, and the parent may then meet with the teacher to discuss the child's progress, using the checklist as a basis for discussion. A brief statement regarding the child's overall progress and potential to adapt successfully to the next level of education often accompanies the checklist. Similarly, in many kindergarten and first-and second-grade classrooms, school report cards are sent home at regular intervals with letter grades or numerical indicators of skill mastery. Many teachers at these grade levels use a checklist format instead of using traditional letter grades to report on the child's mastery of knowledge and skills in prespecified academic and social areas. As with a preschool version, a space or a section for brief comments often accompanies the checklist.

Teachers working with children with identified special needs often use criterion-referenced developmental checklists to assess their development and to determine individual education goals as part of each child's Individual Education Plan (IEP). The checklists are usually based on normative data and have support data on validity and reliability. In addition, they often provide a more detailed breakdown of the skill into subskills than does the "readiness" checklist. These skills, along with a designated level of mastery (80%, 90%, 100%, for example), are often used as goals on a child's IEP. The goals are designed to be reached within a predetermined period of time, often at the end of a 6-month or 1-year period. IEP goals are written cooperatively by the special education teacher, other professionals, and parents. If the child is included in a regular classroom, the classroom teacher is involved.

Expanded Use of Checklists

In recently developed observation systems, such as the Work Sampling System (Dichtelmiller et al., 1994; see Appendix A), teachers are expanding the way they use checklists to document the growth and development of skills over a period of time. Rather than focusing only on whether or not a child has mastered a particular skill, some checklists, when systematically combined with anecdotal records and a child's work samples, enable a teacher to reliably identify other important learning goals as they emerge and become consistent. These goals might include dispositions and feelings as well as knowledge and skills (Chard, 1994). In this way a teacher may guide children toward experiences that challenge them, rather than teaching skills they are not ready to attempt or those they have already mastered.

This use of checklists is consistent with Vygotsky's theory that teaching is most likely to be effective when the teacher identifies the child's zone of proximal development and helps the child to achieve mastery (Berk & Winsler, 1995). In the Work Sampling System the checklist accommodates this new and expanded use of a marking system by providing three choices for each item that correspond to levels of development. The three levels defined in the Work Sampling System are:

Not Yet—The skill, knowledge, behavior, or accomplishment described by
   a Checklist item is not yet demonstrated
In Process—The skill, knowledge, behavior or accomplishment described by
   a specific Checklist indicator is intermittent or emergent and is not
   demonstrated consistently
Proficient—The child can reliably demonstrate the skill, knowledge, behavior or accomplishment described by a specific indicator (Meisels et al.,
   1994, p. 10)

For example, consider the labeled vegetable drawings by 4-year-old
Baxter, a second-year student in Beth Crider-Olcott's multi-age preprimary room. On April 26, Beth's students did representational drawings
of potatoes as part of an investigation of "Vegetables." The children
dictated labels for the parts of their drawings to associate teacher, Sue
Blasco. She labeled the potato drawings for the children who did not have
the writing skills to label their own. In the April 26 drawing of a potato,
Baxter needed someone else to label his drawing for him. At this point
Ms. Crider-Olcott would have marked the Work Sampling checklist item
"Language and Literacy" D-1, "Uses scribbles, shapes, and letter-like
symbols to write words or ideas" as "not yet" (Dichtelmiller et al., 1994,
p. 25). However, in Baxter's May 2 drawing of corn, letters and letter-like
shapes emerged. At this point Ms. Crider-Olcott knew that instruction in
letter formation was within Baxter's zone of development and that he had
a strong desire to learn to make letters. She spent some time helping
Baxter copy letters, showing him how letters are formed. The May 10
drawing with labels shows that Ms. Crider-Olcott's timely instruction
helped Baxter reach a level in a short period of time that could certainly
be called "proficient" (see Figure 5.1).

Another expanded use of checklists is in coordination of programming for children with special needs when a resource teacher comes into
the classroom. Using the same checklist for all children, including children with special needs, facilitates coordination. For example, the teacher
of each child with an identified need for Resource Services can meet on a
weekly basis with the child's classroom teacher to share observations,
monitor progress, and jointly plan practices that will help the classroom
teacher identify the child's zone of proximal development. Using the
checklist as a basis for discussion helps the resource teacher and the
classroom teacher to communicate, since they are using the same terms to
describe the child's development. IEP goals may then be written using
the language of the checklist. This practice is more comfortable for
parents as well, since their child's work is documented and discussed in
much the same way as that of the other children in the class.

Figure 5.1. Baxter's Drawing Labels

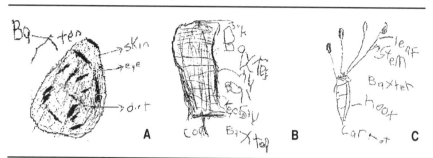

The teacher needed to label this drawing of a potato (A) for Baxter on April 26. Baxter's ability and disposition to label his own vegetable drawing begins to emerge, as seen in his labeling of a drawing (B) of an ear of corn on May 2. Baxter was able to proficiently copy the labels for a subsequent drawing (C).

ANECDOTAL NOTES

Familiar Uses

An anecdote can be defined as a "short account of an interesting or humorous incident"(*American Heritage Dictionary,* 1994). Teachers use these "brief, narrative descriptions of specific events" to develop an understanding of "behavior when there are no other means to evaluate it directly"(Gullo, 1994, p. 72). Perhaps the most common systematic use of anecdotal notes occurs when a teacher suspects that a child is experiencing a significant delay in development, particularly in the area of classroom behavior and/or self-help skills. In this situation the teacher is often asked to document the frequency, duration, and nature of the delay over a period of time. The documentation may be used to make a case for further professional evaluation for the purpose of accessing services for the child. Anecdotal notes are usually a part of this documentation.

Teachers are also familiar with the use of anecdotal notes to communicate with parents. Often a note is written describing an unusual behavior or incident involving the child. A note describing something positive the child has done may be sent home with the intention of building a feeling of esprit de corps between parents and the teacher. Sometimes humorous anecdotes are included in newsletters for parents from the teacher.

Expanded Uses

As teachers become more aware of the importance of documenting children's development, they are expanding their use of anecdotal notes as a way of providing evidence of development. Anecdotal notes may be used as evidence for a profile of the knowledge, skills, attitudes, and dispositions of the child documented in a checklist. Optimal use of these notes requires that several elements be present. First, the teacher should have a "comprehensive and developmentally appropriate picture of what children can be expected to know and do across all domains of growth and learning" (Meisels et al., 1994, p. 8). When firmly grounded in knowledge of child development and the activities typical of a developmentally appropriate classroom, the teacher can have realistic expectations of a child's development in all areas of the curriculum.

Second, the checklist should be in agreement with the teacher's knowledge of child development and curriculum. When this type of checklist is based on a set of criterion-referenced developmental guidelines for which reliability and validity have been established, the teacher can refer to the guidelines when making judgments regarding a child's progress. When making observations and writing anecdotes as evidence of development, the teacher can reflect on these guidelines.

Third, a teacher should plan for the time and materials needed for observing and recording development. It is helpful to gather together and keep handy the materials used to record and organize observations. The longer one waits to record an observation, the less likely one will record it accurately and the more likely one is to forget to record it at all.

Fourth, a teacher should set up a system for regularly observing and writing anecdotes about a child in all areas of development. Then "patterns in behaviors and learning styles" may be revealed (Meisels et al., 1994, p. 8).

When these four elements are in place—(1) anecdotal notes, (2) a checklist that is in agreement with the teacher's knowledge of child development and curriculum, (3) planning for time and materials, and (4) a system for observing and writing anecdotes—a teacher is able to create an ongoing individualized profile of the child's knowledge, skills, and behaviors that emphasizes strengths, progress, and sources of concern. Such a teacher has supporting documentation for planning curriculum to identify the zone of proximal development of each child.

Take, for example, the case of Tyler. In addition to the fact that he was the youngest 3-year-old in Stacy Berg's multi-age prekindergarten class at the Valeska Hinton Center, Tyler had not developed receptive language skills as quickly as others his age. This partially accounted for Tyler's inability to stay focused in many class activities. Ms. Berg and several other teachers had decided to develop projects centering around the theme water. Fish became the focus of the project work in Tyler's room. Ms. Berg noted during the course of this project that a new skill was emerging for Tyler. Referring to her anecdotal notes, which follow, she was able to document Tyler's skill as "in process" on checklist item A-1 in the "Scientific Thinking" section for 3-year-olds: "Uses senses to explore classroom materials and natural phenomena."

> In order to study and investigate a real fish, a large red snapper was brought in for the children to explore. While many children were reluctant to touch the fish, all of the children looked at the different parts of the fish and talked about what they saw. Many children had questions which we were able to answer by looking through our many fish resources. Comments about the fish included the following:
>
> Stacy: What does his eye feel like?
> Tyler: Water.
> Stacy: What is it?
> Tyler: A fish.
> Stacy: Where do fish live?
> Tyler: Water.
>
> In the past during many class experiments and investigations, Tyler would leave the group as the language was too difficult and he could not participate. When the red snapper was brought into the classroom, Tyler voluntarily sat and explored the fish for 20 minutes. With the real object at his fingers, Tyler attempted to participate in the conversation with the other children as he looked and touched the fish.

Because she recognized that Tyler's participation in the group and comments on the red snapper represented "new behavior" for him, Ms. Berg made special note of it by displaying a photograph of Tyler examining the red snapper in the corridor outside the classroom (see Figure 5.2). She further documented the significance of this picture with the written explanation quoted above. This documentation gave Ms. Berg the opportunity to share an awareness of Tyler's emerging skill with others in the school environment so that they, too, might challenge him at his developmental level. At their next parent-teacher conference, Ms. Berg explained to Tyler's mother that he was making progress in language. Using the example of the red snapper discussion as recorded on the anecdotal note to document this point, she discussed with Tyler's mother strategies she

Figure 5.2 Tyler examines and discusses the red snapper firsthand

could use at home to help Tyler develop this emerging skill. As in the case of Ms. Berg and Tyler, by looking for and documenting skills as they begin to emerge, a teacher may discover an area ripe for growth and become more effective by involving others who are close to the child. Anecdotal records may also be used to construct a timeline documenting the development of a skill from the time a child first uses it, through the stages of development, and on to mastery.

Notes on Dispositions

Observations recorded as anecdotal notes may enhance a teacher's ability to follow the child's emotional response to learning by documenting the development of the child's dispositions to play, to work with others, to read, to research, to like school, and to have a sense of competence. For example, consider Jessica, a child in Pam Scranton's multi-age prekindergarten classroom at the Valeska Hinton Center. As part of the "Water" project, the class explored laundromats. Ms. Scranton made the following observations of Jessica's disposition to work with others:

> Jessica has a hard time playing and cooperating in the Family Living Area; she doesn't like to share control of the play sequence. How-

ever, during the course of this project, Jessica has been able to share control and work cooperatively with the other children involved. She was able to offer ideas for the list of materials needed and helped to collect laundry items, even bringing in materials from home.

An example of a disposition leading to a sense of competence can be found in the documentation of the Water Project work that took place in Mary Ann Gottlieb's room:

> Dustin tried several times to trace around the faucet. He was challenged by the uneven surfaces as he tried to trace. However, he continued to work until finally he placed the faucet off the paper and represented it as he perceived it. Dustin's work has become much neater as the Water Project has progressed. He works less rapidly, using an eraser or starting over in order to make his drawings more representational. He is developing the dispositions of independence and resourcefulness.

As they become familiar with the teacher's use of anecdotes to document their child's learning, parents often contribute anecdotes that reveal the dispositions of the child when outside of the school environment. Such information can help the teacher to see whether the growth seen at school is transferring to the home environment. For example, when the Illinois Valley Community College class began their Meadow Project, 3-year-old Brady was inclined to step on the crickets he found. But as the project developed, his mother, Michelle, wrote a note to his teacher to let her know how Brady's attitude toward the insects had changed:

> In our basement there are a lot of crickets. . . . . Brady wants to go in the basement every day to find crickets. He tells me, "Mommy, I go get my friend to put in my bed." I have to try to explain why he can't.

THE PROJECT APPROACH AND OBSERVATION

Project work provides an excellent environment for observing child development, since projects are largely child-directed and teacher-guided. In project work a child selects a question to be answered or a problem to be solved and then, with teacher guidance as needed and/or peer assistance, experiments to solve the problem. Since these experiences are child-selected, they provide the opportunity to see children when they are truly engaged, thereby showing the best of their ability. It is possible to identify the zone of proximal development for children with a wide range of abilities in the context of project work. In addition, since the projects develop over a period of time, they provide the opportunity for many observations of the stages of development of a child's work or dispositions, thereby leading to a very accurate picture of the child's level of development in all domains at a particular point in time and over a period of days, weeks, or even years.

CHAPTER 6

Individual Portfolios: Capturing Children's Competence

Core Items for Portfolio

Individualized Items for Portfolio

Individual Portfolios

Photos, Audio/ Video Tapes

Portfolio: Purposeful collections of work that illustrate children's efforts, progress, and achievements.

—Meisels et al. (1994)

One type of documentation familiar to teachers is the collection of children's work. For years teachers have been saving children's work to share with parents and to use at the end of the year to evaluate a child's progress. Teachers often collect children's self-portraits or writing samples. This type of collection has some of the characteristics of a good documentation process. The work collected is authentic work of the children; that is, it comes from work that children do in the school as part of the ongoing learning process in the classroom. It also enables the teacher to collect work unique to each child as distinct from the standardized responses on achievement or readiness tests. If the teacher systematically collects the children's work, such as self-portraits in the fall and the following spring, the teacher is also able to document observed growth over time. However, authentic assessment systems that meet accountability standards and demonstrate the effectiveness of active, engaged learning strategies, such as those applied in the project approach, require a more systematic approach.

UNDERSTANDING THE USE OF PORTFOLIOS

There are many different approaches to systematizing a portfolio collection process. Gullo (1994) discusses a variety of types of portfolios that have been effectively used in early childhood programs. Some programs use a three-folio system with separate portfolios for ongoing work, current work, and permanently kept work (Mills, 1989; Vermont Department of Education,

1988, 1989). Howard Gardner's (1993) work on multiple intelligences has resulted in portfolio systems focusing on individualized characteristics of students that are revealed when children approach problems and do projects. Gardner also uses the term *processfolio,* which is a portfolio in which the student documents personal involvement throughout the process of doing a project, including planning, interim work, and reflections.

As explained in the Introduction, two of the schools in this book use the Work Sampling System as the primary instrument for assessment. One of the three components of the Work Sampling System is the systematic collection of children's work into a portfolio. According to Meisels and colleagues (1994), "Portfolios capture the evolution of children's competence, providing rich documentation of their classroom experience throughout the year" (p. 13). The purposes of portfolios in Work Sampling include the following:

- Capturing the quality of the child's thinking and work
- Showing the child's progress over time
- Involving the child in assessing his or her own work
- Reflecting the types of classroom experiences available to the child
- Assisting teachers with an opportunity to reflect on their expectations of student work
- Giving students, teachers, families, administrators, and other decision makers essential information about student progress and classroom activities (p. 13)

The Work Sampling System portfolios consist of two types of items: Core Items and Individualized Items. Core Items reflect a child's work across the whole curriculum as well as the child's growth over time. They document student work in five domains of learning: Language and Literacy, Mathematical Thinking, Scientific Thinking, The Arts, and Social Studies. Teachers in a school determine which items they want to collect by identifying particular areas of learning within each domain. They collect the same type of item three times a year. For example, the Core Item for Language and Literacy for 3-year-olds is the collection of a sample of the child's conversation. At the end of the year, the teacher will have three samples of the child's conversation spaced throughout the year. This enables the teacher to see growth. A Core Item collection sheet can be kept on each child so that the teacher knows what has been collected for each Core Item. Some Core Items that these two schools chose to collect are listed in Table 6.1.

In addition to the Core Items for each domain, teachers also collect Individualized Items. These items represent a significant event, an inte-

TABLE 6.1 Work Sampling System Domains

Domain	Sample Core Items*
Language and Literacy	Sample of a conversation (ages 3, 4)
	Sample of a child's writing (ages 3, 4, and K, 1st)
	Record of child's retelling of a story (K)
	Record of a child's understanding of a story from text (1st)
Mathematical Thinking	Record of a child's interest in counting (age 3)
	Record of child's sorting by one or more attribute (ages 3, 4)
	Record of child's patterning (age 4)
	Example of a child using numbers to solve a problem (K & 1st)
Scientific Thinking	Record of a child's recognition of differences and similarities in objects (age 3, 4)
	Recorded questions asked or comments made about the scientific world (ages 3, 4)
	Charts and graphs that were used to collect and analyze data. (K & 1st)
Social Studies	Record of recognition of own characteristics or those of family through drawings or conversation (ages 3, 4)
	Recognition of family or community roles (ages 3, 4, and K & 1st)
	Child-drawn map that indicates child's geographic understanding (1st)
The Arts	Record of child's participation in music, drama, or dance activity (ages 3, 4)
	Record of child's willingness to try different art media (ages 3, 4)
	Record of child's attempt to show feelings or tell a story through art (K & 1st)
	Record of a child's appreciation of the art of others (K & 1st)

In the Work Sampling System, each school or district decides which Core Items to collect at each age or grade level. Items are collected at three times: the begining, middle, and end of the school year. Repeatedly collecting the same items over the year allows growth to be observed.

grated learning experience from multiple domains, or an area of special interest to a child. Although many of the teachers at these schools had previously collected children's work for portfolios, even before the Work Sampling System was adopted for use, they found that the structure of the Work Sampling collection system had distinct advantages. Teachers often do not know what to collect and soon are confronted with a large number of children's work samples and no way to reflect on them in an organized way. Gullo (1994) points out that

> alternative or authentic assessment describes an organizational approach and not a specific procedure. . . . It is an approach to assessment that helps

individuals organize and make sense out of some of the various types of informal assessment procedures. (p. 81)

Restricting collection to a specified number of Core Items and Individualized Items kept the teacher from being overwhelmed by the collection task. Using the specified Core Items for each domain helped the teacher focus on each area of a child's development. This moderated the halo effect, the tendency for advancement in one area of development to influence the teacher's judgment of development in other areas. Limiting the number of items also made the portfolio more manageable when the teacher needed to review and reflect upon children's progress while writing a summary.

Meisels and colleagues (1994) recommend that for a collection process to be effective, items should be informative, easy to collect, and reflective of meaningful classroom activities. At Valeska Hinton Early Childhood Education Center and Illinois Valley Community College, the Work Sampling process of systematic collection and observation is used in conjunction with the project work. The assembling of a collection of children's work for the portfolio was a natural adjunct to the active, engaged learning experiences of the project approach. When children are investigating a topic of high interest, they produce a significant number of high-quality work samples. Many Core and Individualized Items for the portfolio are collected during the projects.

COLLECTING CORE ITEMS

Both of the schools using Work Sampling have classrooms that are multi-age. To simplify the collection of the Core Items in a multi-age setting, staff at the Valeska Hinton Center developed Core Item sheets. Figure 6.1 is an example of a blank Core Item sheet. Teachers tape or staple children's work or a photo to the Core Item sheet when they collect it. If they are writing down an anecdotal note to document a Core Item, they may just write directly on the sheet. There is one sheet for each child for each Core Item. The sheets are color-coded by domain; for example, Language and Literacy Core Item sheets are all yellow, Social Studies are all blue. Each Core Item sheet has a description of the Core Item that needs to be collected and spaces to check other information that the teacher may wish to record.

At the beginning of each collection period (three times a year), the teacher takes the appropriate Core Item sheets that will be needed for all the members of the class, places their names on the appropriate sheets

Figure 6.1 The Core Item Sheet enables teachers to easily collect and record information

Name_____ **Language and Literacy #2 for 3 Year Olds** **Work Sampling System Core Item**	**Valeska Hinton** **Early Childhood** **Education Center**

❑ Fall	Date _____ _____			
❑ Winter	❑ Emerging Behavior		❑ Spontaneous	
❑ Spring	❑ Proficient		❑ Teacher Initiated	

Core Item # 2: **Record of a child's writing** At the three year old level, writing attempts are not conventional. Scribbling and telling someone that it is writing or scribbling letter-like marks are beginning writing attempts. The samples show a beginning understanding of the use of words for communication.

according to their age level, then stacks them by Core Item. While collecting children's work, anecdotal notes, photos of work, or photos of children exhibiting skills, the teacher quickly puts it onto the appropriate Core Item sheet and files it in the child's portfolio or stacks it to be filed later. As time passes, the stack of empty Core Item sheets becomes smaller; there will be fewer and fewer Core Item sheets left to complete. The Core Item sheet reminds the teacher what needs to be collected on each child. When all the empty Core Item sheets are gone, all the necessary items have been collected. This method also makes it easier for teachers when they review the portfolio. Because the sheets are color-coded, they can quickly find all the samples that relate to a particular domain simply by finding the appropriate color. For example, in reflecting on a child's growth in Language and Literacy, the teacher can pull out all the Core Items that are on yellow sheets of paper. Because the dates and other information are in the same place on each sheet, it is also easy to locate the date and put the sheets in order to assess progress.

As classrooms became involved in projects, a side benefit of the Core Item sheets was discovered. They became an efficient way for a teacher to display children's work on a particular project. When used as display items, they facilitated the presentation of the learning that had occurred during the project. Having the Core Item listed on each sheet with an accompanying explanation of the significance of the item in the development of the child provided a ready-made "narrative" to cue parents and others into the learning experience. They also demonstrated how project work coordinated with the Center's curriculum and assessment system and facilitated discussion of children's work with parents and other professionals.

The two Core Item sheets in Figures 6.2 and 6.3 were collected during the blue village's Water Project. Both were used for project displays in addition to being placed in children's individual portfolios. Each teacher used the Core Item sheet in a slightly different way to meet the documentation needs. Pam Scranton collected 4-year-old Veldez's work sample of emergent writing (Figure 6.2) from his play with the water treatment plant that the children had built with blocks. It is a good sample of letter shapes that he had written to facilitate his play. She quickly marked with checks in boxes that this was a new behavior for Veldez and that it was spontaneous. It will be helpful to her later on as she reviews and reflects on his progress for the summary report. She stapled the sample to the Core Item sheet and attached a quick portfolio item Post-it that she had written to remember the significance of the sample. The description of the Core Item on the sheet provided a cue to others as to why the sample was important. It also informed those who might not have background knowledge about the typical development of writing skills.

When teacher Mary Ann Gottlieb collected the Mathematical Thinking Core Item (Figure 6.3) by 5-year-old Tisha, she used the Core Item sheet a little differently. She took a picture as a record of Tisha's counting with one-to-one correspondence. She later typed her description of the event directly onto the sheet and added the picture. This was an efficient way to document a skill that did not produce a product like the previous example.

The next example is a Core Item collected from the Baby Project by teacher Gail Gordon. The first paragraph is the description of the Core Item that was printed on the top of the Core Item sheet. The second paragraph is Gail's words describing the child's behavior that were written directly on the Core Item sheet.

SCIENTIFIC THINKING #1 FOR 4-YEAR-OLDS

Core Item #1: **Record of questions asked and comments made.**

Child verbalizes wonder about the scientific world by asking questions or making comments such as what's inside of something, how does something work, what happens when . . .

After reading the book Baby by Fran Manushkin, Quanisha asked "How do babies get food when they are still in their momma's stomach?" We thought about who would know the answer to that question. She decided maybe her doctor and maybe we could ask him. She also said, "Babies, cry in there."

Figure 6.2 This Core Item Sheet includes a sample of a child's work and a teacher anecdotal note

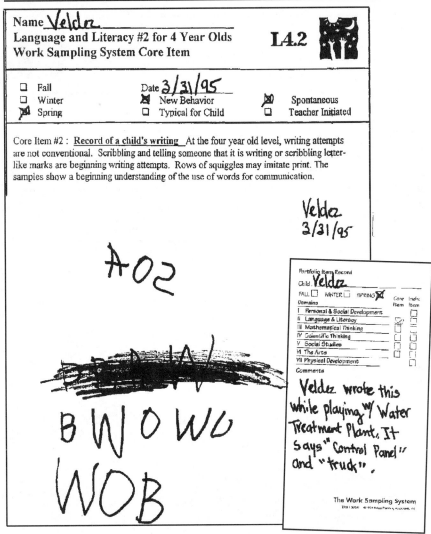

When Rachel Bystry collected the following Core Item during her classroom's Ball Project, she wrote an anecdotal note about what she had observed on the playground. She had simply recorded this observation on a Post-it note designed for Work Sampling collection and checked the domain. She then stuck this note onto the appropriate Core Item sheet:

Figure 6.3 This Core Item Sheet has a photo attached to show the child's participation in graphing

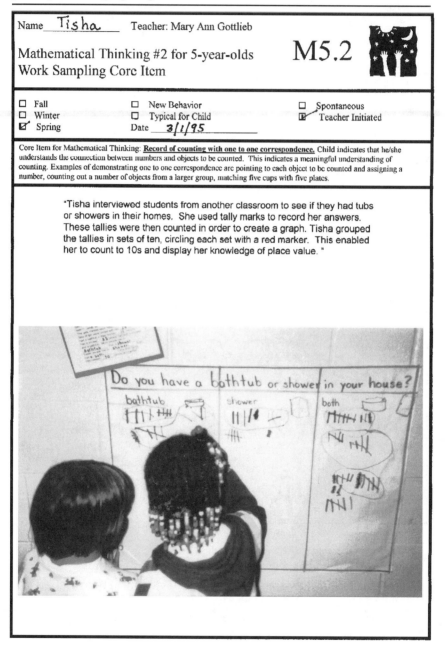

Name __Tisha__   Teacher: Mary Ann Gottlieb

Mathematical Thinking #2 for 5-year-olds   M5.2
Work Sampling Core Item

☐ Fall   ☐ New Behavior   ☐ Spontaneous
☐ Winter   ☐ Typical for Child   ☑ Teacher Initiated
☑ Spring   Date __3/1/95__

Core Item for Mathematical Thinking: **Record of counting with one to one correspondence.** Child indicates that he/she understands the connection between numbers and objects to be counted. This indicates a meaningful understanding of counting. Examples of demonstrating one to one correspondence are pointing to each object to be counted and assigning a number, counting out a number of objects from a larger group, matching five cups with five plates.

"Tisha interviewed students from another classroom to see if they had tubs or showers in their homes. She used tally marks to record her answers. These tallies were then counted in order to create a graph. Tisha grouped the tallies in sets of ten, circling each set with a red marker. This enabled her to count to 10s and display her knowledge of place value. "

Briana dumped bag of balls out on the ground and lined them up from smallest to largest . . . seven balls.

This enabled Ms. Bystry to capture the information before she forgot the event. Sometimes a Core Item will be expanded to provide more information after the teacher has had time to reflect on the observation. This is the Core Item that Ms. Bystry finally inserted into Briana's portfolio:

During outside time, Briana dumped a bag of balls out onto the ground. She was playing by herself and proceeded to line the balls up in order from the smallest to the largest. There was a total of seven balls. She began lining the balls up and switching them one by one. She would switch a couple of balls, step back and look to see if they were just as she wanted them. Briana was engaged in this activity for 15 to 20 minutes.

Teachers have noted that the more interested the children are in the project topic, the better the quality of the Core and Individualized Items. Children are motivated to try new skills and to risk asking for knowledge when they are involved in a project. During project work, the Core Items collected are more often spontaneous than teacher-initiated. This results in identification of more "emergent" or "in process" behavior. And the teacher, being better able to assess where the children are, is better able to plan additional learning activities.

COLLECTING INDIVIDUALIZED ITEMS

In addition to Core Items, Individualized Items are also collected for each child. Individualized items are described in the Work Sampling System (Meisels et al., 1994) as follows:

These items display students' unique characteristics, learning styles, and strengths as well as their integration of skills and knowledge from several domains. A minimum of five Individualized Items is selected each collection period. Individualized Items can represent a significant event, such as the first finger painting of a child who has always avoided messy activities, or a book report on which the student worked particularly hard. (p. 16)

An example of individuality that can be seen in collected work samples is the very different ways in which two 4-year-olds in Michelle Didesch's classroom approached representing a firefighter's hat as part of

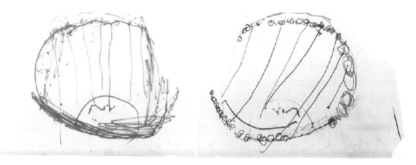

Figure 6.4 Chris's approach to drawing the hat was to draw the front, turn over the paper, and draw the back

the "Hat" project. Ms. Didesch took the following notes on yellow legal pads that she keeps in her classroom for such use.

> Mary and Chris decided to make a fireman hat after firefighters visited our classroom. Chris put the hat on a piece of paper and traced around it. He drew what he saw on the underside on one side. Then he drew what he saw on the top side on the other side of his paper. He included the head straps which had holes in them, the creases (lines) on the top, and the writing on the front [see Figure 6.4]. Mary looked at the shape of the hat, drew it, and cut it out. Then she added a strap so it could fit on her head [see Figure 6.5].

Individualized Items may also be work samples that reflect an integration of learning from multiple domains. Children often work together to produce a product. On a Core Item sheet Monica Borrowman described the writing samples she collected from 4-year-olds in the block area (see Figure 6.6). This sample shows some significant skills on the

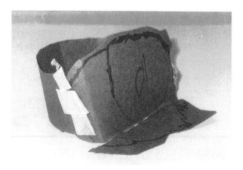

Figure 6.5 Mary drew the parts of the hat, then cut them out to make a hat

part of the children. The cooperation and sharing of the task indicates their level of personal social development, while the work with letters and sounds indicates their level of understanding of literacy.

Often children will become intensely interested in a topic or a particular phenomena that they are observing or studying. They may study it in great depth or at a level of complexity that is not anticipated by the teacher. Work samples and observations of this in-depth study are also collected in the portfolio as Individualized Items. Two Individualized Items were collected from 4-year-old Korey by teacher Judy Cagle during the "Reflections" project. When the teacher provided mirrors and paper shapes for experimentation, Korey produced the work shown in Figure 6.7. Korey observed reflections in water both in natural surroundings and in books. Ms. Cagle asked if he would like to draw a picture of water reflections, and he made the picture "Tree Reflected in Water" (see Figure 6.8). Korey continued to work with this concept, eventually becoming able to make a drawing in which he would correctly look at a shape and determine where the line of symmetry would fall.

OTHER PORTFOLIO ITEMS

Teachers have found that it is often more effective and efficient to use electronic media, such as tape recorders, video cameras, and photographs, to document children's learning. A video can capture movement, children's expression, and light. Videos and photos enable the "collection" of large structures and play environments that children create.

These types of documentation also enable children to revisit experiences and provide a basis for discussing the project experiences and reflecting on what was learned. Children can, in this way, provide their own documentation of experiences. Children can use photographs of field trips to refresh their memory. Photos and videos also enable children to focus on a particular item or aspect of an experience that they may not have noticed when they were on site. Children can be taught to operate cameras and take photos to record information they need later. In Part III readers can see how photos are placed on a planning board for review at the end of a project. Another example of children documenting their own research is shown in Gail Gordon's project narrative of the "Baby" project.

> We went to see the baby furniture so that maybe we could build something for the baby area in our room. We discussed jobs before we left. Ms. Gordon wrote the plans on her clipboard [Figure 6.9]. Then we read the note together and each child copied their word

(Continued on page 70)

Figure 6.6 This Individualized Portfolio Item documents integrated learning

Name __Jessie__
Individualized Item
Work Sampling System Core Item

I

☐ Fall   Date __5-15-95__   ☐ Spontaneous
☐ Winter   ☐ New Behavior   ☐ Teacher Initiated
☑ Spring   ☑ Typical for Child

__Individualized Item.__ This core item represents the uniqueness of the individual child's work.

Jessie, Megan, Nichole, and Nathan built a castle in the block area. They wanted to save it for the next day so they made a sign. " Please save castle." Megan wrote the first word while Jessie sounded it out and told her the letters to write. Jessie continued to sound out and spell. They continued to work together to inventive spell.

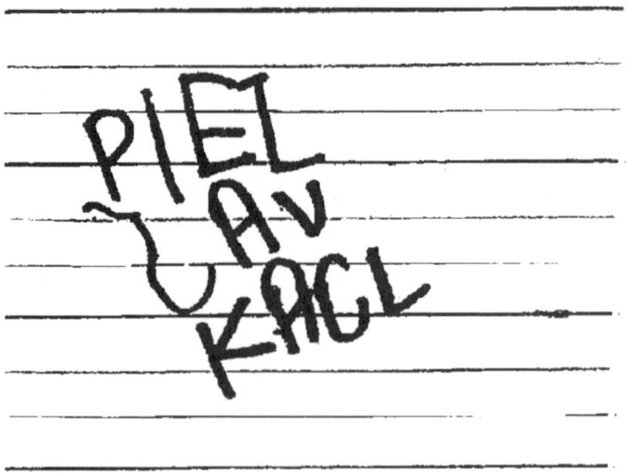

PIEL
AV
KACL

Figure 6.7 The first Individualized Portfolio Item shows Korey's exploration
of a topic

Name *Korey*
Individualized Item
Work Sampling System Core Item   **I**

☐ Fall	Date *March, 1995*	☑ Spontaneous
☐ Winter	☐ New Behavior	☑ Teacher Initiated
☑ Spring	☐ Typical for Child	

<u>Individualized Item.</u> This core item represents the uniqueness of the individual child's work.

*Korey put these half shapes [< ⊦
next to the mirror. He looked at
the shapes and their reflections and
drew what he saw. (See attached
sheet) He drew a line in the
center of each shape and called it
"the mirror line." He discovered
the line of symmetry through this
activity.*

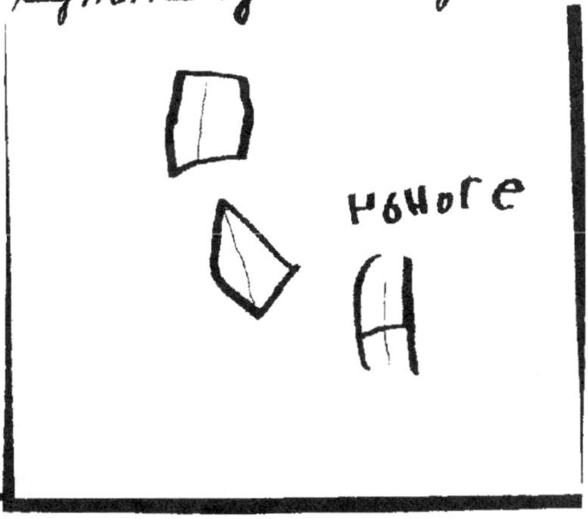

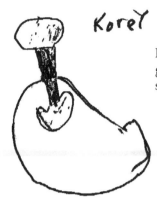

Korey

Figure 6.8 In this picture Korey integrated his knowledge into this representation of a pond

(job) on their clipboard. Ms. Gordon reviewed how to use the camera. Each child took a photo of their item. While they were waiting for their turn, they drew their item on their clipboard [Figure 6.10; Figure 6.11 shows three children's sketches].

Tape recorders also make documentation easier and more efficient. Collecting questions and answers on a tape recorder enables the teacher to reflect on them later and to focus on more than one child. Placing a tape recorder on a table where children are working also enables the teacher to assist other children while still capturing valuable documentation of learning.

All of the types of documentation used for collecting individual portfolios enable the teacher to better assess the child's learning and to plan

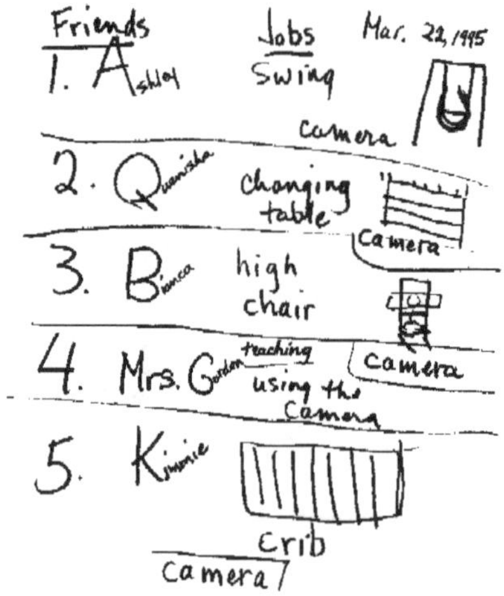

Figure 6.9 The teacher recorded the plans for the trip to the sibling care room

Friends   Jobs   Mar. 22, 1995
1. Ashley   Swing
                          Camera
2. Quinisha   changing
                   table
                          Camera
3. Bianca   high
                  chair
4. Mrs. Gordon teaching Camera
                using the
                   camera
5. Kimmie

                   crib
       Camera

Figure 6.10 Children sketching what they are observing on the field trip

additional experiences based on that assessment. By storing the collected work samples, observations, and electronic media in an individual portfolio for each child instead of a class collection, the teacher is naturally focused on each child's development. The teacher is assisted in focusing on the whole child rather than on development in one academic area by having the portfolio organized so that a specific number of items are collected from each domain. The teacher periodically reviews the children's work in combination with a developmental checklist. This carefully planned, systematic collection provides excellent documentation for making educational decisions and provides a window on a child's development.

Figure 6.11 A child's sketch of a high chair

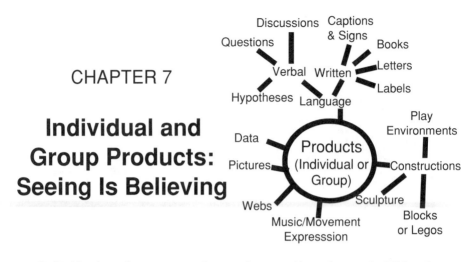

CHAPTER 7

Individual and Group Products: Seeing Is Believing

Individual and group products, the manifestations of children's learning, are perhaps the most obvious and familiar way that teachers document growth. There is considerable potential inherent in products for teachers to reflect on their teaching and to share with others their insights into the growth of knowledge, skills, abilities, and dispositions indicated by the products. Teachers who take advantage of this potential can examine the growth revealed in both the end product and in the process of production.

Writing and art samples are commonly collected by adults as proof of children's learning. However, teachers may find it helpful to broaden the variety of samples they consider. Pictures, webs, musical expressions, constructions, collections of data, and oral language samples are additional products that provide significant opportunities for documentation. Occasionally these products speak for themselves, but generally they are more useful when selected for a particular purpose and accompanied by thoughtful written documentation explaining their significance.

In displays of group work, rather than displaying all of one type of work by all the children in the class, the teacher may find it helpful to display only those products that provide a Window on a Learning Experience, a Window on a Child's Development through participation in the group learning experience, or a Window on Teacher Self-Reflection. Considering each of these windows or purposes for documentation will guide teacher decision making.

WRITTEN LANGUAGE PRODUCTS

Traditionally children's written work is displayed or sent home from school to inform parents of their child's progress in reading, writing, math, and science. However, in some cases these products may be photocopied worksheets or pages from a commercially produced work-

Figure 7.1 "Our Bunny Warren," a sign 3-year-old Jacob created to label
a rabbit warren he constructed as part of a project group

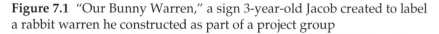

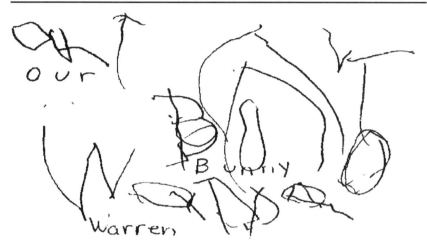

book that contain limited explanation of the significance of the child's
work or the circumstances in which it was produced. These products are
commonly used in American primary schools to document children's
learning.

To provide richer views through the three windows, teachers may
find it helpful to consider using other written language products, including child-made captions and signs, books, letters, and labels.

Signs

For example, as part of their investigation of rabbits, the children of
the Illinois Valley Community College (IVCC) Early Childhood Center
constructed a rabbit warren. Jacob (3.11; i.e., 3 years, 11 months) made a
sign for the front of the warren (see Figure 7.1). By looking at the sign
itself, the viewer can tell that the child is learning many of the conventions of print, such as forming letters, combining letters and spaces, sizing
letters evenly, and orienting letters left-to-right. It is unclear, however,
how much of this knowledge and skill is Jacob's and how much teacher
input and direction took place. It is also unclear whether Jacob was
motivated to write this sign or whether it was a teacher-imposed task.
However, when student teacher Ellen Bejster documented the process
that took place as Jacob wrote the sign, windows were created on three
views:

We began a rabbit warren, made out of boxes, during choice time on Wednesday, November 13. A small group of children were working on the project, measuring and drawing where they wanted the rabbit holes to be cut. . . . On Wednesday, November 20, . . . I asked Jacob if he wanted to write the sign for the warren, and he said, "Yes, I will do it." I wanted to know how well he could print. I gave him white construction paper and a marker and said, "Let's write 'Our Bunny Warren.'" He asked, "How do you spell that?" I began to tell him the letters and showed him where on the paper to start his first word. Jacob knew how to write an "o." I showed him how to make a "u" and so forth on another piece of paper, and he copied each letter I made, one letter at a time. We went through each word in this manner, and he separated the words on his own. Jacob also knew how to make the letter "a" in warren without my help. Chase (4.9), Lewis (3.6), and Amanda (4.4) watched as Jacob made the sign and then we taped it to the warren.

Looking back I could have let more problem solving go on by letting him decide what our sign should say. I feel it was good to work on one letter at a time rather than my writing the whole thing out and letting him copy it. In this way I found he knew there were separations between words and that he did know the letters 'o' and 'a.' I assume he knew this because these letters are in his name.

Ms. Bejster has thus made us aware of the learning experience that motivated Jacob to produce his sign, the amount of teacher support necessary for him to produce the sign, and her reflecting process on the learning that took place. The significance of Jacob's sign and his growth in using written language was enhanced by the addition of Ms. Bejster's documentation.

Signs may convey information in various forms, such as letters, numbers, musical notes, drawings, or symbols. Several large graphs or signs were generated by the first-grade students of Rachel Bystry at Lincoln School in Princeton, Illinois. Ms. Bystry documented the learning of her class as they engaged in an investigation of apples that ultimately led to the construction of an apple store. As part of their investigation, the children generated questions about apples and used them to survey their parents and other children in their K–4 school. They asked their parents questions like, "Do you like apple butter?" "Do you like apple pie?" They asked the other children in their K–4 building, "Which kind of apple do you like best?" The children summarized their findings in two types of large graphs or signs, which they displayed in their classroom. Here again, the teacher's documentation increases the significance of the product to the viewer.

The question was "What color apple do you like best?" Ten said red; five, green; and five, yellow. I told them that 20 people had participated, but the number of people who chose each color was not on the graph. I then asked them if they could figure out how many people had chosen red. There were a couple guesses that were way off, then one boy took a big gasp and said, "I know." Then he told me that 10 had chosen red. I asked him to explain how he had come to that answer. He explained it to the class, and several more hands went up to tell how many had chosen red and green. I was very surprised they were able to understand and read graphs, so I told them I wanted them to try and make their own graphs. They broke up into their teams of five and I gave each group their own original question. None of the groups had the same question as I had represented, and none had the same question as another group. Every group was able to accurately represent their data in graph form! Two made pie charts and two made bar graphs [see Figure 7.2].

Figure 7.2 Pie chart and bar graph by first graders show the result of surveys

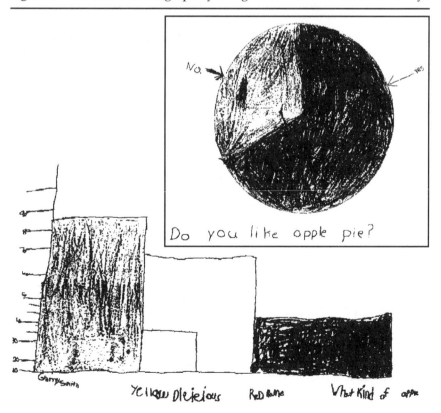

In this case the signs produced by the children were two different types of data collections. In situations like this a teacher can effectively display the signs along with the survey questions that were used to gather the data. By displaying the portion of her journal quoted above, this teacher could provide insight into the accomplishment these signs represent.

Another type of sign to collect as documentation of children's learning is that created by children in the course of their play. For example, Tommy (4.4) produced a chart while working in the writing area of the IVCC Early Childhood Center (see Figure 7.3). He had observed the teacher make several charts and graphs and then spontaneously began to produce his own imitations. Tommy's teacher displayed his chart along with documentation suggesting that the viewer notice the use of both horizontal and vertical drawing, the purposeful variation in size of print, and the use of "white space."

Letters

As with signs and labels, when children write their own letters, the teacher is able to tell a great deal about their knowledge of the conventions of print. For example, Kelsey asked her teacher to help her write a letter to her sister Erin. As Kelsey added thoughts to the letter, it grew until it was several pages in length. The teacher used this letter to provide

Figure 7.3 A chart spontaneously produced in the writing area by a 4-year-old child

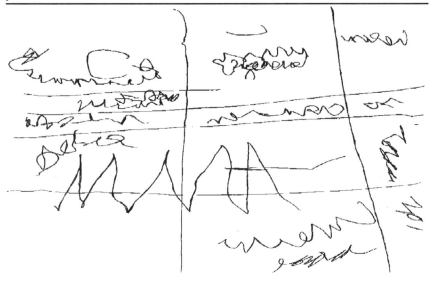

Figure 7.4 Five-year-old Kelsey dictated this letter to her teacher and then copied it

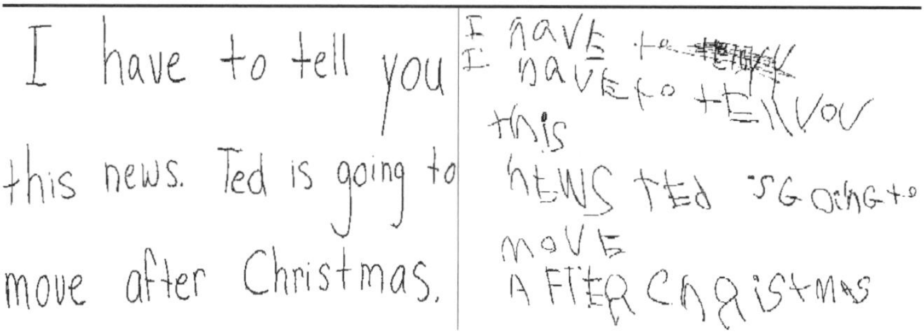

a window on the development of Kelsey's emergent writing, a Core Item in Kelsey's portfolio. A part of the teacher's documentation of the significance of Kelsey's letter went as follows:

> I wrote out the words for Kelsey to copy. A comparison of the following sample of Kelsey's letter with the model I made for her reveals that she is accustomed to using capital "e" and "g" and makes her letters all the same height. She did not include any punctuation, probably because she did not take note of it. Kelsey is aware that words are grouped in a left-to-right progression on lines, but she seems unsure about how many words to include on a line; both "this" and "move" are on a line all by themselves, but the other three lines of her letter contain two to five words [See Figure 7.4].

The teacher filed Kelsey's letter in her portfolio as a Core Item. She might also have been able to create a window on the development of an individual child by displaying a page or two from Kelsey's letter, along with the sample of the teacher's own handwritten example and documentation telling the story of the letter and its significance. Such a display might be used by teachers or other adults to inform their own understanding of the development of writing in children.

Letters written by groups of children can also be used as documentation. Rachel Bystry's first-grade class formed committees to take care of the different jobs involved in creating an apple store. The committees included marketing, advertising, decorating, and construction. These committees produced many kinds of group writing. For example, the members of the advertisement committee wrote their own individual letters and then combined them to form a computer-written letter to parents to ask for donations (see Figure 7.5). The teacher might make

Figure 7.5 A rough draft by two members of the first grade advertisement committee *(left)* and the full committee's final letter *(right)*

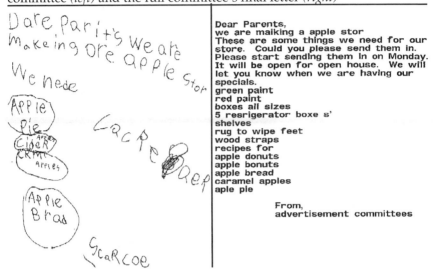

Dear Parents,
we are maiking a apple stor
These are some things we need for our
store. Could you please send them in.
Please start sending them in on Monday.
It will be open for open house. We will
let you know when we are having our
specials.
green paint
red paint
boxes all sizes
5 resrigerator boxe s'
shelves
rug to wipe feet
wood straps
recipes for
apple donuts
apple bonuts
apple bread
caramel apples
aple pie

From,
advertisement committees

effective use of these products by creating a display in which the preliminary letters by several of the individual children are displayed along with the final group letter. The teacher could also display an explanation of the process the children went through to integrate their letters into one.

Books

Helping children to produce their own books as a group or as individuals has become increasingly common as early childhood teachers have come to value providing children with opportunities to use emergent writing in meaningful context. These books provide not only an indication of the level of the child's developing literacy skills, but also a window into the child's knowledge, ideas, and dispositions.

Sean is a very verbal child who is working on writing stories and maintaining one constant theme throughout the story. He wrote a story to sell in the apple store we had constructed in the classroom. We read the story together, then he told me what the story was about. We took the story he had written and reworked it so everyone would understand what he was trying to say. The story is about two apples that were friends and grew on the same tree. One apple was picked and the other left behind. The apple that was left was then chosen by another person, and in the end the two apples were placed by one another and were happy again. Sean uses a lot of invented spelling in his writing and has wonderful ideas for his books.

Here again, including the ages of the children involved, the context or learning experience within which the book was written, and any pertinent teacher reflections can be a useful accompaniment to documentation of such products.

As part of their investigation of rabbits, preschoolers in Sallee Beneke's multi-age prekindergarten class wrote a book about the ways in which the class rabbit and turtle were the same and different.

> I wanted the children to think in more detail about the rabbit, so I decided to present the possibility of a Venn diagram at circle time. I laid out a circle of yellow yarn to stand for Sweetie (the rabbit) and a circle of red yarn to stand for Franklin (the turtle). I explained that the area in the middle where they overlapped was a place for us to put those things that we knew were the same for both Franklin and Sweetie. Then, as each piece of knowledge was brought forth, I wrote it on a Post-it, along with a quick symbol for the idea, and asked the children where the Post-it should go on the diagram. As the diagram filled, it occurred to me that the same thoughts would make a great book. I said, "Hey! Does anybody want to work on making a book out of these ideas during choice time? If you do, I will help you." Mary Kate, Jacob, Marissa, Emma, and Amanda all came to work on the book at choice time. Each of them had definite ideas about which page (Post-it) they would like to make. I wrote out the words of the page, and they provided the illustrations. Later in the day some of the children moved back to the diagram and copied words from the Post-its directly onto the diagram. Mary Kate copied three of the Post-its. This was the first time I observed Lewis attempting to copy letters. I had to assist him "hand-over-hand." He was very pleased that he had written on the diagram just like Emma and Mary Kate. The next step may be to see if any of the children would like to revisit the book and write their own words this time.

In this case, the documentation explains the significance of the process that led to the final product. The teacher might use the children's book, along with a narrative somewhat like the sample above, to explain the growth and problem solving that took place during the production of the book. A copy of this book and the narrative could be included in each child's portfolio, and a display of the same material would open a Window on a Learning Experience for adult visitors and colleagues.

VERBAL LANGUAGE PRODUCTS

Children's verbalizations about a topic can provide insight into their knowledge, skills, and disposition to learn. In the past, early childhood teachers often documented a child's ability to recite memorized materials such as nursery rhymes, fingerplays, and chants. As with written language, teachers may find it helpful to expand the types of verbal products they document, thereby providing a richer view through the three windows. Other verbal products might include hypotheses or opinions, stories, discussions, or questions.

Hypotheses

For example, second-grade teacher Dot Schuler found that she could learn a lot about the knowledge of her class by listening to and recording their statements or hypotheses:

> Robert wrote in his journal about a bluff. He read it to the class, as well as my written response, which was, "What is a bluff?" Here are the responses he got.
> 1. A big, old rock and dirt and rocks and leaves on it. (Ross)
> 2. Rock. (Matt)
> 3. A half of a mountain. (Scott)
> 4. Shells pushed up against each other for thousands of years (that's what my dad told me.) (Sarah)
> 5. A worm in a rock for thousands of years. (Brittani)
> 6. Lava explodes and makes hard rocks. (Troy)

In this short sequence Ms. Schuler found out not only what individual children didn't know about bluffs; she also found out a great deal about what other related concepts these individual children do have about rocks and rock formation and how they are integrating these concepts.

Discussions and Questions

Discussions and questions are also valuable verbal language products. By recording conversation among a small multi-age preschool group as they planned and constructed a giant cocoon, Sallee Beneke found evidence of their developing knowledge of measurement in inches.

Teacher: Now, how much blue do you want?

Marla: Twenty inches, I think.

Teacher: Twenty inches. OK, let's measure. Let's start with this piece. Do you know what 20 looks like? See that's 20 right there [points to 20 on the yardstick]. OK, and there's 10. Look here, this is 20 inches from here [points to end of yardstick] to here [points to the 20]. Is that enough?

Marla: Yah, 20 inches.

Teacher: So you only want this much, from here [points to beginning of paper] to here [points to 20 as it lines up on the paper].

Emma: Actually, from there to here [points to other end of yardstick].

Teacher: Ohhh, that would be 36 inches.

A verbal language sample like this would be a good item for the portfolio of each child involved, and it could create a Window for Teacher Self-Reflection if used to provide the catalyst for discussion in a staff meeting on teaching technique. When displayed in the same area as the end product the children were creating during the recording of the conversation, the sample could open a Window on a Learning Experience.

After Mr. Vaughn, from Bradford city maintenance, gave the children a tour of the town water tower, pump room building, and reservoir, Kim Fisher's first-grade class held both small-group and large-group discussions about their findings and what they could do with those findings.

> The following day I met with small groups of children in the hallway and discussed the information they brought back from the trip as well as what they would like to show about what they learned. We discussed art, writing, drama, construction, and mathematical possibilities. As the children came up with ideas, we wrote down the idea as well as the materials that they might need. We met again as a whole class to discuss materials that the children could try to bring in. Over the course of the discussions, there were some disagreements about information that the children collected as well as several new questions. Several children thought Mr. Vaughn had said that there were snakes in the reservoir. Since this is drinking water, they were very concerned. Lillie is a next-door neighbor to Mr. Vaughn, so she set up an appointment with him and interviewed him in regard to the students' questions, then returned to class with the answers:
>
> - *How does the gas get out of the water in the reservoir?*
>   The water hits the metal plates, sprays into the air, and the gas leeches out of the water.

- *What if someone fell in the reservoir?*
  No one is allowed near the reservoir. That is why it is surrounded by a tall fence with barbed wire at the top. If someone did fall
  in, we have to try to reach in and get them out or call for help.
- *Why do we drink the reservoir water if there are snakes in it and how*
  does it get clean?
  The reservoir water is clean already because it comes from an
  underground well that is tested to make sure that the water is
  clean. There are no snakes in the reservoir water. (It was the pool
  water that the snakes could get into.)

Ms. Fisher has created a Window on a Learning Experience by documenting the process through which she was able to listen to and evaluate the
direction of the project work for both individuals and the class as a whole in
developing their investigations. She has shown how through discussion she
was able to help small groups of students decide on projects that reflected
their interests, and she was able to capitalize on disagreements and questions
to extend students' problem-solving skills and knowledge of the topic. She
has demonstrated the value of children's verbal language products by
recording and documenting them in context. She has shown how valuable it
can be for teachers to listen to discussion and to use disagreement to promote
problem solving and investigation.

WEBS AND LISTS

Webs

Webs are also products that can be used to document children's
learning. Webs can serve as a way to group small lists. They make it
possible for children to visualize the relationship between categories and
subcategories. They help children to visualize a point in a meaningful
context. For example, several small groups from Sallee Beneke's class
took walks through the meadow behind their preschool to make observations. As each group returned from their walk, the teacher read the items
recorded on the web by the previous group, and they were able to
compare what they had seen with the observations of the previous group
and make additions to the web. One group saw a large spider with black
and yellow on its back, and they added this information to the spider
section of the web (see Figure 7.6).

Webs can be adapted in several ways to reflect growth in the children's
knowledge. For example, when Kim Fisher led a first grade class in their

Figure 7.6 A small groups of children returned from walks in the meadow, they added their observations to this web

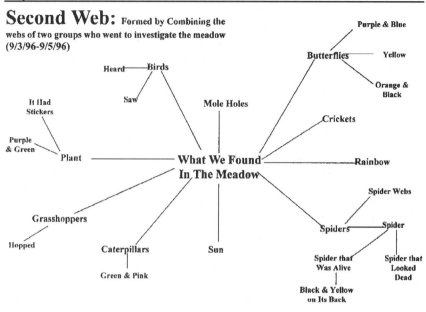

Second Web: Formed by Combining the webs of two groups who went to investigate the meadow (9/3/96-9/5/96)

Heard ———— Birds

Saw

It Had Stickers

Purple & Green

Plant

What We Found In The Meadow

Mole Holes

Purple & Blue

Butterflies ——— Yellow

Orange & Black

Crickets

Rainbow

Spider Webs

Spider

Spiders ——— Spider

Grasshoppers

Hopped

Caterpillars

Green & Pink

Sun

Spider that Was Alive

Spider that Looked Dead

Black & Yellow on Its Back

investigation of water, she found that color-coding the items on the web that were added on later dates helped her to keep track of additional ideas:

> Concluding that we knew quite a bit about water, we made a classroom web of everything that the children could think of about water. The original web was written in black. As our study of water continued, the children thought of other things that could have been added to the web and those ideas were added in orange.

A display including the web done at the beginning of the project and the web done at the end of the project can make a strong statement about knowledge gained over the course of a learning experience.

Lists

Like a web, a list can be a useful grouping of related information and can reveal much about the knowledge, skills, and dispositions of those who author it. When the process of preparing the list is also documented, the potential of the list to inform through the three windows becomes even richer. Lists are often prepared by small groups of children as a step in completing a project. For example, Mary Jane Elliott, a kindergarten teacher at the Hong Kong International School in Hong Kong, comments on a list generated by her students as they brainstormed a list of ingredients for apple cake:

> The decision on how much of any ingredient to add was based on their previous experience with baking, bits of wisdom they remembered hearing from their parents, and the "team" effort at figuring out how to proceed. "We'll put in half a cup of sugar, because too much sugar isn't good for you!" "Let's put in 1 cup of milk, because milk is good for you." "We only have four apples left. Let's put them all in." (This was the last day of our project, so that seemed very reasonable. This cake was to be eaten at the final celebration.) When the eggs were added, the first child said to put in one egg, but another child said, "My mom always puts in 2 eggs in cake." No one made any comment contrary to that, so 2 eggs went in. One-third cup chopped butter went in only because it was so difficult to get out of the package and off of the spoon. Initially the children had selected 1 cup for the butter, but the situation dictated that only one-third went in. I had about 1 cup of M & Ms and 1 cup of chocolate chips in a bowl. Most of the M & Ms were put in the batter and a big handful of chocolate chips. Giggles and laughs accompanied their addition to the batter. No little cookies were available, so that ingredient was left out. No one seemed concerned. The big cup (1 cup) was used for flour. Half was added at first and then more. One of the boys commented as he was stirring, "This is beginning to look like cake batter."

As the children prepared their recipe, they revealed their understanding of relative amounts of ingredients that go into a food they commonly eat, their knowledge of units of measurement, and their disposition to be flexible and to work as a team. By displaying the conversation that took place as the children prepared the list, along with the list of ingredients, the teacher can create a window on a learning experience.

PICTURES

"Any and all forms of purposeful visual expressions, beginning with controlled scribbling" can be defined as "picture making" (Mayesky, 1990, p. 165). While picture making is usually a part of the curriculum in most American early childhood programs, considering children's pictures in terms of their potential for documentation may help the teacher to create views through the three windows. Teachers may find it helpful to document and evaluate them in new or additional ways. They might ask themselves:

- What was the meaning of the work for the child?
- What integration of knowledge and skills did the picture show?
- Was the child attempting to represent something, or was the child using drawing symbolically?
- Did the child engage in problem solving in the production of the picture?
- Did the child revisit an earlier picture or attempt to revisit the picture of another child?"

Representational Pictures

An example of thinking about children's artwork as representational can be found in the following reflection from Sallee Beneke's journal. This reflection was used to document a portion of the mural that was produced by her multi-age preschool class as part of their Meadow Project.

Today I set up the overhead projector in the hallway and tacked the partially finished mural to the wall. I had used the copy machine to create transparencies of the children's meadow and insect drawings, and children were invited to choose, project, and trace the drawings of their choice onto the mural. Chase, who has shown little interest in drawing, came out to see what was going on. Emma was adding her daisies to the mural. He watched as I moved the transparency around on the overhead and scooted the projector in and out to and from the wall, asking Emma where she wanted the daisies to be on the picture. He watched Emma trace her daisies and was excited by the process. Soon he said, "I want to draw on there!" so I gave him a transparency and told him to go to the project area and draw something from the meadow. Emma left and I walked over to see what he was doing. He was slowly drawing a circle. It was not a relaxed, smooth line. He was working so hard at it that some parts weren't curved. We went back to the projector, and I asked him where he wanted his drawing to be placed on the picture. He pointed to the side of Emma's flower and said, "Right here, It's an egg sac." Jacob was watching, and I asked him if he'd like to put one of his drawings on the picture. He had several. He chose a drawing that he had earlier called a beetle. It had six legs. When I asked him where he wanted to place it, he said, "On Chase's egg sac. It's a spider." I said, "But yesterday you told me it was a beetle because it had six legs." Chase agreed with Jacob that it was a spider. I said, "Well, I'll make it go on the egg sac, but I'm not sure it's a spider." Jacob transferred the beetle picture onto the mural, looked at it, and then said, "I know! Just a minute." He ran into the room and came out with several of the plastic creatures from the sand table. He found the beetle and counted its legs. He took the plastic spider with him to the mural and added a leg onto each side of the beetle. "There," he said. "Now it's really a spider." Chase watched closely throughout this process and would point out his egg sac and the spider to anyone who came by. This was a very exciting part of my day. I could almost feel the learning in the air. This was my first observation of Chase using and naming representational drawing, and both Chase and Jacob demonstrated that they were integrating knowledge about the meadow. Jacob and Chase both demonstrated a disposition to work together, and Jacob showed his ability to do research and self-correct.

As noted in the journal entry, children's knowledge and skills are reflected in several ways in this example. By displaying this journal entry and the drawings of Chase, Emma, and Jacob alongside the mural, all three windows are opened. As the reader follows Chase and Jacob through the process of combining their contributions to the mural, a view is created on the individual development and dispositions of the children. Similarly, by displaying this journal entry with the mural, a window on the value of the production of the mural as a learning experience is created. Other teachers who read this entry while examining the mural may use it to reflect on their own teaching and documentation skills.

Another example of representational drawing can be found in the Bradford first-grade Water Project. Teacher Kim Fisher describes the learning experience that led up to the drawing:

> Once the idea for the field trip was discussed, we began thinking of things that we would like to find out on the field trip. After quite a bit of discussion, the children compiled the list of questions. At this point, we talked about the need for each person to be responsible for finding out some information at the field site, so that when we got back, we could put everyone's information together and learn a lot. The children volunteered to ask the questions on the list. Each wanted to find the answers to their own questions and, usually, someone else wanted to help them. We wrote names by each question so we could remember who was responsible for what [See Figure 7.7].

Figure 7.7 Kyle's drawing and text provide information about the water tower to share with his class

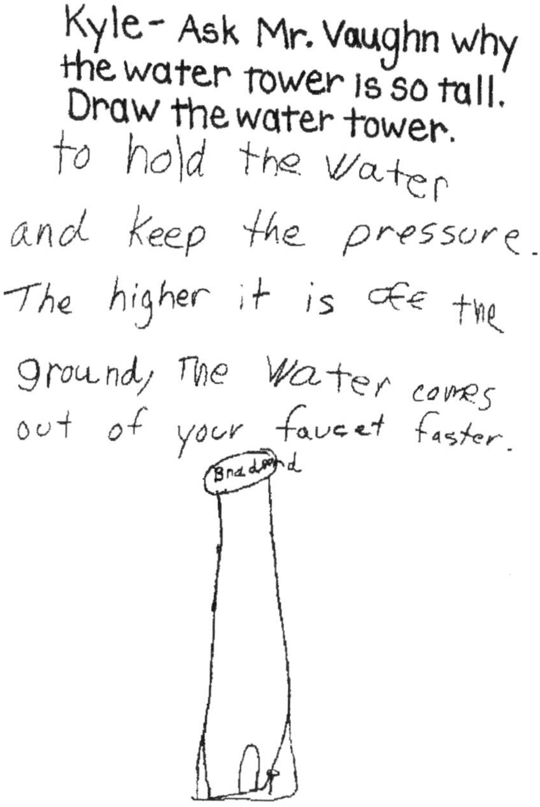

Kyle- Ask Mr. Vaughn why the water tower is so tall. Draw the water tower.
to hold the Water
and keep the pressure.
The higher it is off the
ground, The Water comes
out of your faucet faster.

As in the case of Kyle and his drawing of the water tower, displaying a narrative explaining the circumstances leading up to the drawing, along with the drawing, serves to heighten the viewer's awareness of the importance of the picture and draw the viewer's attention to the child's knowledge as revealed in the detail of the picture.

Time 1 and Time 2 Pictures.

Teachers can create strong documentation of growth in knowledge and skills by displaying pictures in which the child has revisited an earlier topic or by displaying a picture to which the child has directly returned to do editing. Such a display is sometimes called a display of

Figure 7.8 The growth in 4-year-old Marla's knowledge of butterflies can be seen in the difference in detail between her 9/24 and 10/1 drawings

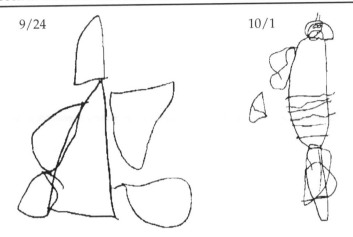

9/24   10/1

Time 1 and Time 2 drawings. For example, consider two drawings by 5-year-old Marla (see Figure 7.8). In Marla's Time 1 picture on September 24, the butterfly has only two sections to its body. It has four wings, a body, and a head. However, by October 1 (Time 2) Marla has learned so much about butterflies that she is able to represent them in much more detail. She has communicated her knowledge of the antennae, eyes, three body parts, four wings, and six legs (drawn as lines across the abdomen). By sharing or displaying these two drawings as a set, the teacher can open a window on a child's development by providing strong documentation of Marla's growth over time.

When a narrative account is added to the display to explain the context within which the Time 1 and Time 2 drawings were produced, all three windows are opened. For example, in the Bradford first grade Jordan created two different drawings of a fence (see Figure 7.9).

Another thing the children enjoyed doing was making sketches. One day, while waiting for their project to dry, Jordan brought a sketch of the swimming pool fence and Brittany brought a sketch of the water tower to show me. After admiring their sketches, I asked if possibly they would like to look at the photographs of the fence and water tower on display at the back bulletin board. I suggested they might find even more details to add to their pictures. After looking at the photographs, they asked to take the photos to their desks. After a

Figure 7.9 Drawings of a swimming pool fence by Jordan. She drew the first picture from memory; the use of reference pictures helped her to show great improvement in the second drawing

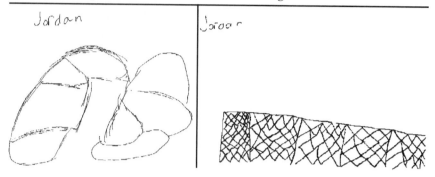

while, they brought second sketches to me that incorporated the details from the photographs.

Jordan's Time 1 and Time 2 drawings, along with the journal of her teacher, provide a window on Jordan's development, a window on the learning experience within which this kind of growth can take place, and a window for teachers to reflect on their own classroom-management techniques and use of reference materials and drawing in the classroom. This method of redoing a task does not always have to repeat the exact same task. An example of slightly varying a task but still providing evidence of growth is the series of vegetable pictures shown in Chapter 5 (refer to Figure 5.1).

Symbolic Pictures

Sometimes children draw to symbolize something rather than represent it. Maps and diagrams are an instance of this. Or they may use symbolic drawing to depict something that is not visible to the eye or is an abstract concept. The *American Heritage Dictionary* (1994) defines symbolism as "the representation of things by means of symbols." Symbols themselves are defined as "something that represents something else by association, resemblance, or convention." For example, when Ms. Fisher's class went on their field trip, Ashley's assignment was, "Ask how water gets to school." Ashley symbolized her knowledge by drawing the school and the watertower, and then connecting the two locations with pipes. However, Ashley has never seen these pipes. She only knew of their

Figure 7.10 Ashley's drawing symbolizes her understanding of the way the pipes take water from the water tower to the school

existence from the explanation given by the water-tower caretaker (see Figure 7.10). Symbolic art can be used to document learning in the same way that representational art is a product that can open a window on the development of an individual child.

Children can use symbolic drawing to represent their knowledge of relationships in space. After a field trip to the grocery store, children in Val Timmes's multi-age primary class created floor plans to use in the construction of a grocery store in their classroom. They symbolized the location of shelves and aisles with the use of simple lines. Their intent was not to represent them as they really looked, but rather to symbolize them in order to show their location (see Figure 7.11). By displaying these floor plans along with a narrative describing the events that led up to the drawing, the teacher can create a Window on a Learning Experience as well as a Window on a Child's Development .

Children sometimes use symbolic drawing to represent things that are abstract concepts to them. Kim Fisher's first-grade class generated a list of questions that they had about water.

The children were asked to select a question and develop a hypothesis to answer it. Jordan selected the question, "How do you get waves to move in the water?" and she prepared a drawing to explain her hypothesis, which was "The wind." In her drawing Jordan used a line to symbolize the force of the wind (see Figure 7.12).

Figure 7.11 A first grader's floorplan for the class grocery store uses lines and spaces to symbolize placement of the various departments and aisles

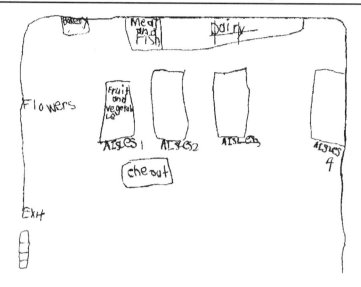

Figure 7.12 First grader Jordan used a diagonal line to symbolize the wind pushing against the water to form waves

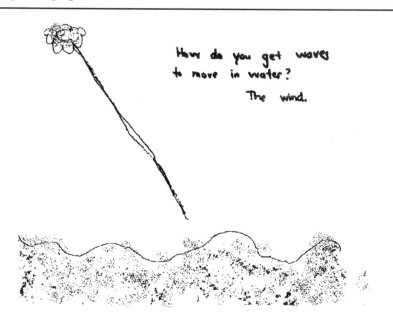

MUSIC AND MOVEMENT

Music

Although difficult to convey in writing, it is important to note that music and movement are also significant products of children's learning. This journal entry from her teacher documents that as 4-year-old Kendra became increasingly engaged in the Meadow Project, she began to sing about it:

> Early this morning Kendra, who was sifting rubber insects out of the sand at the sand table, began to sing about the meadow! It was really something! I had a soft jazz piano playing on the CD player, and I was working in the writing area when I heard her start. It was really kind of a beautiful, soulful kind of warble, a little like a blues piece. It really didn't seem as if it could come out of such a small body. I turned on the tape recorder and asked Mindy to take it over close to her, but the only word I could make out was "meadow." There may not have been any other words. It seemed to be purely a revelation of Kendra's feelings. What was also interesting was that soon other children around the room began to sing. It was almost like hearing birds gradually awakening and joining in, in the early morning. One thing is for certain: Kendra was definitely a leader in this. She knew how to express her feelings about the meadow in music, and the others imitated her. My interpretation of this phenomenon is that with their singing, the children who sang revealed their positive feelings about the beauty of the meadow.

The tape recording of this musical product provides documentation of Kendra's disposition to sing, her disposition toward the meadow, and her ability to lead. Teachers can record samples of music such as the one described above and can use them to provide a window on the development of an individual child or a window for teacher self-reflection if the tape is shared with colleagues. A teacher might also provide the child with an opportunity for self-reflection by playing the music for the child.

Movement

As with music, it is difficult to record movement, other than by anecdotal record, videotape, or frozen moments in time that are recorded in photographs. Particular topics, however, lend themselves to imitation by movement, and in the course of this movement children often demonstrate knowledge about the nature of the subject they are imitating. For example, Kendra, who showed her disposition toward the meadow in her singing, showed her knowledge of the of butterflies through her movement. Kendra darted back and forth as she ran and would frequently lower herself to the ground to "suck the nectar," then she would be up and running again. She would run faster when other children called out, "Look out. There's a bird!" Kendra's movements revealed her understanding that butterflies suck nectar from flowers and that birds eat butterflies. Her movements also revealed the degree to which she had mastered skills in gross motor development, such as agility, speed, balance, and coordination, and her disposition to use them for her own purposes.

CONSTRUCTIONS

For the purposes of this book, constructions can be defined as three dimensional representations created by children. Children can represent their learning through many kinds of constructions. Three types of constructions that will be described here are play environments, sculpture, and constructions using blocks or building toys.

Play Environments

Play environments are a wonderful source of evidence of children's learning. Here again, a great deal can be learned by examining the end product, by observing the problem solving and social interaction that takes place in the process of construction, and by watching the children as they play in the construction. In creating their own play environments, children replicate what they are aware of and what they consider to be important. The detail which they add to their constructions often provides evidence of the depth of their understanding.

For example, small mixed-age groups composed of prekindergarten, kindergarten, and first-grade children worked together on the construction of a hospital at the Valeska Hinton Center. The groups had made a field trip to the hospital, and each group was in charge of bringing back field sketches of a particular department. In the following days the groups used their field sketches to construct the various departments they had visited. An elevator, waiting room, gift shop, patient room, x-ray department, and obstetrics department were all constructed and then joined to turn the wide school hallway into a large "hospital." The details that these children included in their constructions were documentation of the knowledge they had gained. For example, in Figure 7.13 we

Figure 7.13 Play environment created as part of the Hospital project, showing a patient room and the radiology department

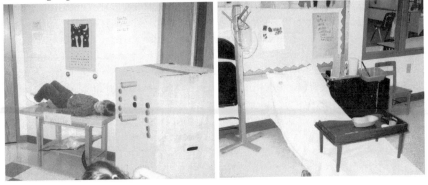

see the "patient room," which includes adjustable bed, tray, remote control, IV bag, "Get Well" card, water pitcher, and x-ray department in action. Note the x-ray machine in the background, which was constructed by one team of children. They have shown their knowledge in the dials, tubes, "electrical connection," and sign that says "x-ray machine."

The construction of a play environment can pose many problems for children. They must work in three dimensions and must decide which materials will work best for them as they move from the planning stage through final construction. In referring to the physical properties of different media as they relate to a child's decision making, George Forman (1994) explains that "a transformation in the medium that a child can easily produce is an affordance. Each affordance provides the child with a method to express an idea by transforming the medium"(p. 42). As young children develop a construction, they must deal with the affordances of the materials they have initially selected to use in communicating their ideas. Children often want the construction not only to look "real" but also to function like the "real thing." For example, as the Lincoln School first graders constructed their apple store, they had to solve many problems, including the "problem of the shelves." Teacher Rachel Bystry observed and described the problem-solving process and the learning that ultimately took place as follows:

> When we started to build our apple store, several boys got excited about building shelves out of cardboard that had been brought in by parents. They cut several long pieces, painted them green, and started taping them together. The first shelf they built had two sides and

a top, but it wouldn't stay up. The boys were frustrated, but they knew that we were having an engineer come and visit, and they believed he could help. The engineer was brought in to talk to the children about planning before building. They asked him how to build shelves out of cardboard, and he really didn't have a specific answer, but he told the children that triangles were very strong structures. That afternoon the boys got back together, took their shelves apart, and started over. They rebuilt the shelves using triangles to support the top [see Figure 7.14]. They also stacked the shelves two- high. They looked great, and the boys were excited about their structure. The next day they started placing some of the apple merchandise on the shelves, and they kept collapsing. I then noticed the boys taking the shelves apart and asked why. Zack, one of the builders, said, "The triangles worked better, but you can't build shelves out of cardboard. You need wood or metal or something stronger."

This group of boys ultimately built their shelves out of wood, but in the process of experimentation they learned a lot about the affordances of cardboard and the physical ability of various shapes to support weight. They learned to use an expert as a resource, and they displayed great persistence in the course of their experimentation. The teacher documented this by creating a wall display that included photographs and a description of the hypothe-

Figure 7.14 These first graders tackled the problem of building shelves out of cardboard for their apple store

sizing, experimentation, and reflection which took place. This display could be used to open all three windows on learning.

The grocery store constructed by Val Timmes' multi-age K–1 class grew out of an investigation of fruits and vegetables. Their construction was elaborate and included many reproductions of food items as well as furnishings. As the children played in the grocery store, they revealed their knowledge of the function and roles of store employees, the use of the store equipment, and the variety and categories of food and other products. For example, children stocked shelves, ran groceries over a "scanner," and sacked groceries. As the children paid for their groceries and received change, they demonstrated their knowledge of currency and numeracy (see Figure 7.15).

Sculpture

Sculpture is defined as the "art or practice of shaping three dimensional figures or forms" (*American Heritage Dictionary*, 1994). Children construct sculptures with a variety of materials. Examples are clay, paper, wire, wood, and cardboard. But whatever materials the child chooses to use, the child's experience or inexperience with the medium must be taken into

Figue 7.15 Children in a multi-age K–1 classroom play in the classroom grocery they have constructed

account and included in the use of the child's sculpture as documentation of learning. For example, 5-year-old Marla, in Sallee Beneke's mixed-age pre-kindergarten class, was able to include several details in her drawing of a butterfly (refer to Figure 7.8). But when in Marla's first experience with clay she chose to create a butterfly, the result was extremely simple, a body and two wings. Given additional experiences with clay, Marla was able to create a clay butterfly with head, thorax, abdomen, four wings, six legs, antennae, and eyes. As Marla revisited the topic in this medium, her knowledge began to emerge.

Small three-dimensional sculptures from materials other than clay might include representations made from paper, cardboard, wire, or any combination of the three. Pictured in Figure 7.16 is a lobster constructed from paper, cardboard, masking tape, a toilet paper roll, and pipe cleaners. It was created by two children in Val Timmes's class for their grocery store. In the play environment, the lobster was kept inside a glass aquarium. The children had observed and sketched the lobsters in the tank on their field trip to the grocery store. The sculpture reveals the children's knowledge of lobster anatomy. For example, they have included antennae but not eye stalks.

Large sculptures are sometimes created by one or more children. For example, one of the culminating activities in the "Meadow" project at the

Figure 7.16 One of two lobsters constructed by a small team of children for a classroom grocery store project

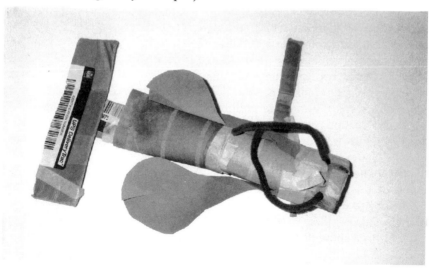

IVCC Early Childhood Center was the construction of what the children called "the giant butterfly." The length of the body was greater than 6 feet, while the wing span was greater than 8 feet. In the process of creating this butterfly, the children used many skills and solved many problems. This anecdote from Sallee Beneke's journal provides an example:

> The chicken wire form for the head was shaped separately from the larger piece, which was to become the abdomen and thorax. When the time came to join the head to the body, one of the three children working on the sculpture that day wanted to center the head on the top of the body. Jacob (3.11) insisted that the head belonged on the end of the body by the thorax, and finally made his point when he went to the table and got a book with a picture of a butterfly to support his position.

From her observation of the children as they solved this problem, the teacher could tell that Jacob understood the relation of the body parts of the butterfly and that he was able to use reference materials. His disposition to convince the other child with factual information rather than force was also documented in this example. The teacher could use this example to open all three windows.

Blocks or Building Toys

Observation of block play and block structure provides early childhood teachers with an understanding of children's knowledge of math and physics concepts. Block structures can also represent children's knowledge of a topic. Children often bring other materials into the sculpture to add interest or detail to their representation. For example, three boys in Pam Scranton's multi-age preprimary class at the Valeska Hinton Center became interested in constructing a model of a water treatment plant. Their class had looked at reference materials, interviewed an expert, and done preliminary sketches. The boys worked on their construction over a period of days, and incorporated found objects, such as egg carton cups, milk jug lids, and paper towel tubes to represent parts of their model. The completed construction included a parking lot, control panel, and treatment pools (see Figure 7.17). The boys labeled many of the parts of their construction, so the end product provided evidence not only of the knowledge they had gained about water treatment but also of their writing skills.

Children show us in many ways that they are learning. They produce verbal and written language, pictures, webs, music, and a variety of

Figure 7.17 This photograph reveals the detail in this block construction of a water treatment plant constructed by a small group of 3- and 4-year-old boys

constructions in which they represent their ideas, thoughts, and feelings. Teachers can take advantage of this wide array of products to assess the development of their knowledge, skills, abilities, and dispositions. In looking at the products of children's learning, it is important that we examine and document not only the end product but also the problem-solving and learning that took place in the process of production. Thoughtful documentation of the products of children's learning can open a Window on a Child's Development, a Window on a Learning Experience, and a Window for Teacher Self-Reflection.

CHAPTER 8

Self-Reflections of Children: Thinking About Thinking

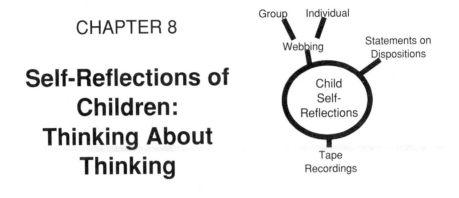

Child self-reflections are statements children make that reflect their own knowledge or feelings. These statements can provide a record of the child's emotional and/or intellectual involvement in a project. A record of children's words can be handwritten, audiotaped, or videotaped and can serve a variety of purposes. The form in which the self-reflection is presented is best determined in relation to the window the teacher hopes to open by using it as documentation.

REFLECTING ON THEIR OWN WORDS

Just as it is sometimes helpful to teachers to reflect on their own teaching by reading their journal entries, watching themselves on video-tape, or listening to a tape recording of their interactions with children, it is sometimes helpful to children to reflect on their own words. Children are interested in examining their own ideas as they have previously expressed them. An astute teacher will notice and record statements children make that might provoke new or continued interest in a learning experience if reintroduced at a later time. For example, as the children in Sallee Beneke's prekindergarten class met to plan a construction that would show what they were learning about butterflies, she was able to refer back to an earlier statement by Marissa:

Teacher: Marissa, You told me Monday that you thought we should make a "giant cocoon." Do you still think that's a good idea?
Marissa: Oh yes!

Teacher: Well, would you like to tell everybody else what you were thinking on this?

Marissa: Oh, yes. Well, I was thinking that we could build a really, really big cocoon.

Teacher: What do the rest of you think?

[Many statements of agreement and further contributions of ideas followed. A list of materials necessary to construct the cocoon was generated by the children.]

By referring back to Marissa's earlier statement, the teacher showed respect for the thinking of children and maintained a sense among the children that they were in control of their own learning. Marissa was given the choice of agreeing with or rejecting her earlier suggestion (to build a giant cocoon). Because she had this choice, she had the opportunity to reflect on, or think critically about, her own idea. The other children were free to agree or disagree with Marissa's idea, which provided them, too, with an additional opportunity to engage in influencing the course of the learning experience.

Teachers who are selective in collecting children's own statements or words and presenting them to the children can guide the course of the learning experience without predetermining it. They can do this by listening with a critical ear to the children's words and by recording and presenting in verbal form those statements that, in their judgment, hold the most potential to maintain child interest in the project and present the most possibilities for extending or deepening the richness of the learning experience. For this purpose teachers will often collect and store short statements or even whole conversations that seem to have potential, even though they may not know exactly how they will use them.

SELF-REFLECTIONS OF DISPOSITIONS

As discussed in Chapter 1, children's words often reveal their dispositions toward themselves or others. Statements made by a child that reveal his or her "habits of mind and action" (Katz & Chard, 1989, p. 30) often begin with the word "I." Examples would be statements such as "I really like my school," "I was there first," or "I will get you a Kleenex."

A teacher who is interested in collecting self-reflections of dispositions can make a conscious effort to develop the habit of listening for "I" statements. A collection of these kinds of statements can provide a record of a child's developing character. For example, as the children in Sallee

Beneke's class prepared to paint a giant papier-mâché butterfly that they had constructed, she asked for volunteers to create "plans" for the color scheme of the butterfly. The three volunteers were given simple paper silhouettes of a butterfly shape and asked to bring them to the teacher when they were decorated. The volunteers were free to use any of the materials available in the art area in their "plan."

> Jacob (3.11) came out into the hall with his butterfly plan and said, "I'm going to paint part of this butterfly pink." I said, "But, Jacob, there's no pink on your plan." Jacob said, "OK, I'll fix it." He went back to the art table and returned in a little bit with a piece of pink tissue paper glued onto the middle of his plan. He said, "Now I am ready to paint." He was surprised when I said, "Jacob, we don't have any pink paint." Then he suggested that we make some. The children got so interested in the pink paint that soon we had to bring a gallon of white paint into the project area so that the children could mix white with each of the colors. Jacob surveyed the excitement and declared, "I think I must be a genius to think of this!"

This teacher was able to add this statement to Jacob's portfolio to provide a window on a growing disposition to have confidence in his own intelligence and ability to solve problems. She also created a Window on a Learning Experience by creating a display near the completed giant butterfly featuring Jacob's statement and pictures of the children mixing the paint. The display provided the viewer with insight into the sense of control over their own work that the children felt and so helped to show the source of the sustained persistence and dedication that could lead 3- and 4-year-old children to create and complete such a complex and beautiful construction.

In making this display, the teacher has provided a window on the relationship of dispositions to a learning experience not just for those outside the learning experience to see in, but also for the use of those directly involved to reflect on their own experience. Children are often the most frequent viewers of this type of documentation. They use the display to revisit and reflect on moments or experiences that have meaning for them. The documented statements allow children to ask adults to join them in discussing these moments, which sometimes leads to a discussion among adult/child, adult/children, or child/child as to which dispositions helped the children in their work. A variation on such a display might be to copy and reduce it and include it in a scrapbook format.

SELF-REFLECTIONS OF A LEARNING EXPERIENCE

When children are interested in a learning experience, vocabulary and concepts from the experience spontaneously begin to enter their conversations. For example, 6-year-old Kylie's statements to a visitor about preparations for the class apple store revealed her involvement with the learning experience:

> "Well, our apple store is fun, but it's a lot of work," she said, sighing. "Of course the boys have been doing the heavy work because they *think* they are stronger than the girls." She rolled her eyes. "The girls have been making lists about what kind of things we want to sell in our store. I like green apples," she said.

These comments, as described by the visitor, reflect both the child's interest and intellectual involvement with the apple store project. A teacher can draw a great deal from a statement like this and can document the fact that the child understands the nature of the work that will need to be done and is actively engaged in planning and decision making in the work. The statement demonstrates that the child feels a sense of ownership in and responsibility for the project. Social interactions are taking place in the course of the project, and the child sees herself as part of a team effort. Although she questions the boys' claim to strength, an assumption that work should naturally be divided along gender lines is also implied in her statement. The documentation of this statement has opened a window for the teacher to see that children in her classroom are dividing tasks according to gender stereotypes of strengths and abilities. Research has indicated that the teacher needs to challenge such bias with an active/activist approach (Derman-Sparks, 1989). Documentation of children's self-reflections not only enable the teacher to see bias problems but also can enable the teacher to monitor changes in understanding and practice.

Kylie's self-reflection also provides evidence that she feels challenged by the project but that the challenge is within her zone of proximal development and that she is gaining content knowledge. In other words, the teacher can provide a Window on a child's Development that documents not only the child's knowledge but also her ability to integrate it with other skills and apply it in a setting that requires problem solving (construction of the apple store.)

A perceptive teacher may lead a child to reveal the extent of his or her knowledge through self-reflection. Lee Makovichuk, a teacher in Edmonton, Canada, recorded such a conversation with 5-year-old Richard as he constructed a bird-feeder:

> At the carpentry area Mike and Alysson join in, eager to help with the construction of the bird-feeder. Verbal exchanges happen as the children look at and choose the appropriate materials. I become an observer, as tools are organized, materials decided on, and the work begins.
>
> Richard pauses. "I think I'm the boss."
>
> "Oh, how's that?" I ask.
>
> Richard responds, "Well, I have the plans and I know what needs to be done, so I think I could be the boss."
>
> "So you're the foreman," I reply.
>
> Richard pauses. "No, I'm the Threeman."
>
> As I process this information, Richard notices Alysson has left the worksite. "No, I'm the Twoman," he says.
>
> "Okay, Twoman, what do I do?" I ask.
>
> Richard directs me to hold a piece of wood on a piece of linoleum as he traces it. Mike suggests he is to cut the linoleum and produces scissors. Together Richard and Mike struggle with the scissors and linoleum, then decide to use a saw. They place the linoleum in the vise; Mike holds the linoleum while Richard saws it. Together we continue to work, nailing the linoleum onto the piece of wood. Once this task is complete, Mike leaves in the direction of the snack table. I ask, "Twoman, what's the next step on your plan?"
>
> Richard replies, "I'm not the Twoman anymore, I'm the Oneman."
>
> Confused, I ask, "What makes you the Oneman?"
>
> Richard explains, "Well you see . . . I only have one person now."
>
> "I see two—you and me," I respond.
>
> "Well, I can't work for myself so I count only you," Richard replies.
>
> Understanding is confirmed. I understand Oneman Richard. Smiling, we continue our work.
>
> I choose to support Richard's thinking in regard to quantifying objects (people) and subtraction of real objects. Later, in a subtle approach, perhaps with a story or visitor, we will clarify job titles. . . . I really feel the understanding of quantifying real objects was the task at hand; had I corrected his misunderstanding, I would have missed the opportunity to witness the level of his understanding of quantification.

Self-reflections of engagement with a learning experience can be documented for the child's portfolio or can be effectively displayed by mounting them along with photographs of the child participating in the work. Viewing such documentation may stimulate the child to think reflectively about her participation in the learning experience and may provoke the child to become more deeply involved.

GROUP AND INDIVIDUAL SELF-REFLECTIONS

The statements children make as they present their thoughts for addition to a group or individual list or web often provide the teacher with a rich sampling of self-reflections. These are self-reflections because they require children to reflect on their own knowledge of a topic, recognize that it is knowledge that they have gained, and then express it so that it may become part of a web or a list. For example, at both the beginning and the end of a project, the teacher often records the children's level of knowledge of the topic under investigation. When compared, the differences in content revealed in the statements recorded on the two webs will reflect growth in the children's knowledge over the course of the project. For example, in the initial web created by Kim Fisher's first grade class as part of their investigation of water, the children included wash face, wash food, drink, wash hands, wash hair, brush teeth, wash TV, swimming, wash rocks, flush toilets, wash glasses, wash cars, ice cubes, wash cats, wash dogs, water plants, soap and water, wash clothes, take a bath or shower. A list dictated to Ms. Fisher by the group toward the end of their Water Project reveals both the narrowing of the focus of the group's investigation to an investigation of the water tower and significant growth in knowledge and vocabulary.

NEW VOCABULARY: reservoir, water pressure, valve, coupling
NEW INFORMATION:
- Pipes break when water freezes and expands, breaking the pipe
- The height of the water tower creates water pressure.
- The water tower is blue because that's the color the citizens of the town chose.
- The distance around a pipe is its circumference.
- The silver thing on the outside of the water tower is an exhaust fan. The pumps run so much pumping the water to the top of the tower, that a fan has to take the heat out of the pump room.
- Water from an underground well is treated, put in a reservoir to

remove gas, pumped to the top of the water tower, and then piped to our homes and school.
- Pipes vary in diameter, length, and the material that they're made of, according to their function.
- What it means for something to be "to scale."

Mary Jane Elliott, a kindergarten teacher at the Hong Kong International School in Hong Kong, recorded the self-reflections of her students as they brainstormed a recipe for apple cake. Here are a few excerpts from her extensive notes presented in Chapter 7.

- We'll put in half a cup of sugar, because too much sugar isn't good for you!
- Let's put in 1 cup of milk, because milk is good for you.
- We only have four apples left. Let's put them all in.
- When the eggs were added, the first child said to put in one egg, but another child said, "My mom always puts in two eggs in the cake." No one made any contrary comment, so two eggs went in.

In this description it is apparent that the children had some knowledge of the kinds and amounts of ingredients that belong in a cake. They also have a strong self-awareness that they do, in fact, have some knowledge about baking. Ms. Elliott attributed this to "their previous experience with baking, bits of wisdom they remembered hearing from their parents, and the 'team' effort at figuring out how to proceed." While the individual statements could certainly be used to create a window on the development of each of the individual children involved, a collection of a set of statements made as a group generates a web or list, such as those shared by Ms. Elliott, that can be very useful in creating a Window on a Learning Experience. Effective teachers often display a selection of such statements along with the web or list that was the primary product of the children's work. This type of display documents the kinds of thought processes and problem solving that resulted in the product.

Many audiences benefit from a view through this window. While visitors to the classroom might see the value in the approach to teaching that the teacher is using, a parent might see the contribution of his or her child to the learning experience. For example, Bonnie Grusk, a parent of twin girls, Mary and Emma, in the IVCC early childhood program, wrote the following note after reading the documentation of the Meadow Project. The documentation featured Emma's self-reflections, which were recorded as she worked as part of a small team.

The feelings I have had about the progress the girls have made in getting along and working together were reinforced when I read about the children working in teams. They are experiencing what it means to be part of a community; and what better time to learn about getting along and about the importance of cooperation than at the age of 3 and 4. Mary and Emma have always been a team of sorts; when you're a twin I believe that just comes with the territory. It is a different type of team now; they listen to each other and really take into consideration what the other has said and/or may be feeling.

By documenting the child's self-reflection, the teacher was able to provide the parent with a Window on a Child's Development that the teacher had observed in the classroom. In turn, this provided an impetus for the parent to think about the child at home and to share her observations with the teacher.

Teachers viewing the same display might read the documentation and use it to think about how this child's self-reflection reveals how the experience encouraged growth in working together. This would be especially meaningful if the teacher would add the parent's thoughts to the display. When children read self-reflections of other children, they are encouraged to reflect on their part in the learning experience. When two or more children view this type of display, they can discuss and critique the work of the group and gain insight that will help them to be more productive in the future.

When the viewers of such documentation are nonreaders or early readers, it is particularly helpful to display photographs taken of the children as they shared their ideas. Photographs take the children back to the moment of the learning experience and put print displays, such as lists and webs, into context. Once the list or web has been read to the children, along with the self-reflections which are displayed, they will likely remember the experience, and spontaneous discussing and critiquing of the work will take place, as it would with older children who read.

An outcome of this type of documentation, then, may be that children become interested in revisiting the experience that is documented and improving on their earlier work. By documenting their statements, the teacher can provoke the interest of the children in expanding on and extending earlier work.

As children talk, we find out many things about them. Statements of self-reflection are of particular interest because they provide insight into the child's dispositions and engagement in the learning experience. Selections of these statements can be used to provide others with a Window on a Child's Development and a Window on a Learning Experience as a whole. The teacher who presents documentation of their self-reflections in such a way that children can further reflect on their own words creates potential for children to evaluate their own work and provokes them to revisit and extend their earlier work.

PART II

Learning How
to
Document

CHAPTER 9

Organization and Presentation of Documentation: Opening the Window

open: —*tr.* . . . . 11. To reveal the secrets of; bare. . . . —*intr.* . . . . 3. To spread apart; unfold. . . . 4. To come into view; become revealed. . . . 5. To become receptive or understanding.

—*American Heritage Dictionary* (1994)

The recent interest in the outstanding early childhood education provided by the Reggio Emilia schools of Italy (Katz & Chard, 1996) has focused attention on the importance of documentation. Many teachers have been impressed by the documentation displays of children's work that have traveled the world in the Hundred Languages of Children Exhibit. This has encouraged teachers to attempt to document learning occurring in their own classrooms. It is advisable for the teacher who is attempting to increase his documentation of children's work to approach the process as if he were learning a new skill, such as driving a car. As in learning to drive, the first attempts are slow and each step has to be carefully considered and planned. Integrating comprehensive documentation into a classroom is also a skill that takes time to learn. A driver eventually becomes so skilled and confident that she can drive without consciously thinking about most of the separate tasks, like starting the car. The teacher who works at improving documentation eventually finds that documentation is such an essential part of his teaching that it becomes automatic. This chapter provides assistance for those first steps into increased documentation. However, the teacher will discover many more from his own experiences and from sharing with colleagues.

GETTING READY TO DOCUMENT

Gathering Materials and Equipment

A teacher can prepare for the documentation process by gathering together materials that are helpful for documenting. These include Post-it notes for writing down observations and folders for collecting children's work and anecdotal notes. Some teachers find it helpful to place pens and notepads around the classroom so notes can be jotted quickly without having to leave an area where children are working. The availability of a clipboard for every child assures that children's thoughts and representations will be captured on field trips and during in-depth investigations of topics in the classroom.

A camera with film is very useful. Any camera with a flash that the teacher feels is easy and comfortable to use will work; however, a 35-mm camera with film speed of 200 will result in good inside and outside shots on the same roll of film. Teachers will want to try different types, speeds, and brands of film to see what works best in their classroom. A zoom feature will enable closer shots without intruding on children's work space. Be sure that batteries are fresh for taking inside shots.

A tape recorder that is small and can be placed inconspicuously near children working will help capture conversations. Recorders with a detachable microphone enable the teacher to place the microphone in the children's work area but to start and stop the recorder from a distance. It is important to try out the tape recorder to see if it can record over the high noise level in an early childhood classroom.

Using a video camera at certain times during a project enriches the documentation. The high noise level in the early childhood classroom also affects videotaping. It is helpful if the video camera also has a detachable microphone. The camera needs to be easy to carry and use and to operate without extra lights in situations of low-level light.

Access to a photocopy machine enables a teacher to copy children's work that they wish to take home, reduce and enlarge samples so they can be more easily displayed, and make multiple copies of children's books or project history books for children to check out and share at home. A computer with a simple desktop publishing program will enable the teacher to make displays and narratives that look professional. A scanner can greatly simplify the process of making books, displays, and newsletters. It enables the teacher to directly scan children's work into the computer, reduce it so that it is manageable, and share it in a variety of ways. If a multimedia computer system is available, the teacher, older children, or a parent can produce their own multimedia record of projects.

The importance of this material and equipment in the schools of Reggio Emilia is seen in this statement from Vea Vecchi (1993), *atelierista*, in the Diana School:

> Yet, this method takes much time and is never easy. And we know that we have
> much to learn. The camera, tape recorder, slide projector, typewriter, video

camera, computer and photocopying machine are instruments absolutely indispensable for recording, understanding, debating among ourselves, and finally preparing appropriate documents of our experiences. (p. 122)

There is no doubt that all of this material and equipment is helpful. They encourage documentation because they enable the teacher to be more efficient and the documentation to look more professional. However, many teachers begin documenting with just a spiral notebook, some notecards, an inexpensive camera, and an organized system for collecting children's work.

Many teachers find it helpful to make multiple copies of blank forms with a list of the names of all the children in their class. The forms can have names down one side and blank columns. When the teacher needs to observe or assess whether each child has mastered a specific skill or concept, she can write the concept in one of the columns and check it off or write a date observed in the square by the child's name. An example of this would be to have a form listing the names of the colors. These are also useful when the teacher wants to collect the same thing from each child, such as in Core Items for a portfolio.

Identifying Curriculum Objectives

In preparing to document, it is also important to obtain a copy of the goals and objectives and any curriculum guides. If the teacher is documenting for program evaluation or to demonstrate accountability, he will want to focus on the knowledge, skills and dispositions that the school district or early childhood program wants children to develop. This will not only focus the documentation but also increase teaching effectiveness. If there is no required curriculum, a teacher might find this information in a purchased curriculum guide, report card, or developmental checklist. If the school uses standardized, group-administered achievement tests, it is important to be aware of the content and skill objectives on which the test is based. These can be found in the manuals for the standardized test.

Once goals and objectives are identified, the teacher can think about what types of documentation would best provide evidence of achievement of these goals. For example, if the objective is for children to be able to meaningfully count five objects by the time they leave a 4-year-old prekindergarten program, a teacher could then look at the web showing types of documentation (refer to Figure 3.1) and think of the types of documentation that could provide evidence of the ability to count to five. Possible documentation might be an anecdotal note of a child's participation in the process of counting the number of children at a table for snack or a dictated narrative about a block construction in which the child counted the blocks. Anticipating the need for documentation by making a list of knowledge or skills to be documented will make this easier. A teacher can also make signs with this information and place them in the classroom where he can see it and remind himself of what to collect.

This may be especially helpful in assuring others that the teacher will be addressing this list of goals and objectives, even though she may be teaching in a different way from her colleagues and may be using more direct, active, or interactive experiences as described in Chapter 1.

Planning for Documentation

It may be helpful for the teacher to review the web of types of documentation in Figure 3.1. This will help to keep in mind the variety of ways that he can document and then plan for collecting the documentation. Many teachers find it helpful to incorporate plans for documenting in their written lesson plans.

Another consideration in planning is for the teacher to try to anticipate what she may want to do with the documentation. For example, if a teacher makes an observation that will go into a portfolio as a Core Item, it may be easiest to record that directly on a Core Item sheet instead of on a Post-it note. It is important, however, not to be too narrow during the collection process. Documentation is often used for several purposes later in a learning experience, so sometimes it is better if the documentation is saved in a format that is easily adapted to a variety of uses.

Another consideration in planning for documentation is to capture evidence of children's knowledge and skills at the beginning of an ongoing learning experience such as a project. Having children make a web or a list of what they know about a topic provides a written record. Some teachers plan on students adding to or altering the web as the learning experience progresses as a visual record of their learning. Recording or writing down the exact words of the children in statements and questions at the beginning and end of a learning experience also enables assessment of change in vocabulary and understanding.

Setting Reasonable Goals for Documenting

When teachers are first focusing on documentation in their classroom, they often make the mistake of thinking that everything that occurs in the classroom must be documented. It is easier if a beginning documenter focuses on one or two domains. A teacher can identify one or two things that he will collect and when he will collect them throughout the school year. Writing samples are a good place to start. Another way to narrow the focus is to set a goal of documenting one learning experience from beginning to end, such as a project or a unit.

Another fairly common mistake that is easy to correct is trying to capture all learning in photographs or to photograph activities for which other documentation has already been gathered. Again, it may be helpful for the teacher to revisit the web to see the variety of ways besides photographing that children's learning can be documented.

Other reasonable goals that a beginning documenter may choose are setting aside a certain time to observe each day, focusing observations on one child per day, or focusing observations on one child in one area daily over an extended period of time. As the teacher becomes more adept at documenting, she may set goals to increase documentation, such as increasing observations of children's learning in a particular area of the room.

Anticipating displays

It is at this time that a teacher might also need to think about what kinds of displays will result from a learning experience or from documentation of a particular area of learning. This is a good time to revisit the windows framework in Chapter 2 and to project what audiences might be viewing the displays. The teacher can ask herself if the purpose of the display is to provide a Window on a Child's Development or to share a learning experience such as a project. It is also helpful to think about what different points of view the audience for the display is likely to have.

PREPARING CHILDREN FOR DOCUMENTING

There are many advantages to involving children in the documentation of their own learning. In preparing for documentation, and even during documentation, the teacher can focus some time on preparing children for documentation. She can introduce and directly teach skills that children may need to document their own learning. One of these skills is using a web to record what they know and then what they have learned. Another skill is using writing to record their thoughts. Even preschoolers can help make lists of materials needed. Teachers can model questioning and hypothesizing so that children learn how to phrase questions for research. The questions and answers can then be documented. Practice in construction skills such as taping, stapling, and building things will enable children to better represent their knowledge through making products.

Children can be involved in developing and monitoring their own portfolio. According to the *Teacher's Manual of the Work Sampling System*

(Dichtelmiller et al., 1994):

> For students reviewing work provides an opportunity to reflect on what has been occurring in the classroom and what they have been doing and learning. Looking at work reminds students of the experiences that led to the creation of the work. Reviewing their work helps children see the changes they have made since the beginning of the year and to develop a sense for how much they have grown. (p. 74)

As in all areas of documentation in which they participate, it is important for children to have easy access both to materials and equipment to document and to storage places for their items. Milk crates with hanging files are popular with many teachers for portfolios because they encourage student involvement in the collection process.

It is important that children also understand that they should be encouraged to express what they are learning in many ways. In addition to webs and lists, types of documentation that they can understand and readily use are narratives such as conversations, written stories, and books; writing such as captions and signs; constructions such as block structures, play environments, dioramas, and models; and artistic expressions such as drama, drawing, painting, sculpture, musical expressions, and photography.

Children should be encouraged to do as much writing and drawing as possible about what they are observing and learning. Keeping their clipboards readily available for independent use supports their drawing and writing. The teacher can encourage them to revisit, redraw, and rewrite. This helps children solidify knowledge, become aware of their own learning, and demonstrate to others the extent of the learning occurring during a project or other experience. If these items, showing first attempts (or sketches) and final copies, are displayed prominently, then this documentation can be very powerful.

DOING THE DOCUMENTING

When the teacher begins the documentation process it may, once again, be helpful to review the web in Figure 3.1 to keep the variety of ways to document in mind.

Recording and Reflecting

There are two processes that the teacher has to work into her schedule when documenting. One is time to record information and collect children's work; the other is time to reflect.

It is easy to assume that recording and collecting will happen throughout the day; however, it is important that the teacher carefully consider how this process will occur. As noted previously, placement of recording materials (notes, pencils, tape recorders) is critical because the teacher does not have time to stop and search for them in the middle of teaching. An excellent plan is for the teacher to simply record thoughts in a spiral notebook as they occur throughout the day. Many teachers take time each day to outline what was done that day. This may focus on the class, an individual child, the project, or the teacher and the teaching strategies.

Another time can be set aside daily to summarize and reflect on the observation data and items collected. Documentation can guide the teacher in planning what resources to access, experts to bring in, or field experiences to be initiated. Any skills identified as needing to be taught can also be planned for other teaching times.

It is helpful for the teacher to watch for opportunities to collect documentation of several children at one time. Recording and transcribing a conversation and making multiple copies of the conversation provide documentation of the language skills of each of the children involved in the conversation.

Photographing

Often teachers are disappointed in the quality of the photographs they take when documenting. Morgan and Thaler (1996) give some simple rules that can result in more interesting and effective photographic documentation.

In selecting the view to be photographed, it is important to see the scene as the camera sees it. People have selective vision; cameras do not. Clutter, dirty dishes, flashy bulletin boards that are not noticed in real life seem to dominate when the photograph is developed. The teacher can look at the background through the camera, then reposition himself so that the picture has fewer distractions. Or the teacher can get closer to the children or activity being photographed so that they can fill the picture and block out the background.

Photographs of large groups of children or posed photographs do not show enough detail or children's expression to provide evidence of learning. The focus should be on small groups, individuals, and candid shots.

Photographing at different angles can be effective. For example, a child working on a structure might be photographed from above, showing the top of the structure, then at the eye level of the child.

Composition can pull viewers into the story being documented by following the rules of thirds:

> Just imagine your viewfinder has two sets of parallel lines going through it; two running horizontally above and below the center and two running vertically to the right and left of center. Each pair of lines divides the frame into three equal parts, hence the name the rule of thirds. If you frame your pictures so that . . . your children are located where any two lines intersect, or along any of the lines, the picture will be more visually appealing . . . more natural and lifelike, and the photo will be more interesting if you point the lens below their heads. That way, their faces will be in the upper third of the frame. (Morgan & Thaler, 1996, p. 27)

The rest of the photo can show the child's work or project.

Remember also to take photographs that tell a story. It is helpful to take a series of photographs, especially when there is problem solving and building and construction going on. This can show the thought processes of the children and enhance everyone's understanding of what occurred. Examples of a series of photos are shown in the Mail Project Memory Book in Part III. It can be very valuable to involve children in photographing their own work.

Tape Recording

Tape recording, video or audio, provides wonderful opportunities to capture what is occurring. They are helpful for documenting children's learning and for a teacher's reflection on his own teaching. Capturing conversation accurately in a busy early childhood classroom is assisted by using equipment that allows the teacher to separate the microphone from the recording equipment. Putting a recorder in place and letting it record is simple and can be effective. It may also be helpful to have small group or individual activities set up in an area in the classroom where there is less noise or even to use a section of the hallway or a conference room. It is especially meaningful for children to tell about their work and to have their narrative taped.

Webbing

Webbing can occur with the whole class, during small-group times, or with individual children. The value of the record that it provides is increased when it is revisited and revised, so it is important to provide opportunities for that to occur. One method that some teachers have found productive is to photocopy the first web and keep it; then add to the original and copy it again, and copy that one, and so on. The series of webs shows the growth of knowledge and understanding.

At the end of each project, the teacher can go back to her list of required content. After making a copy of it, she can highlight all those content objectives covered in the project work. Displaying this list prominently with other project documentation will help others viewing the documentation to see the relevance of the work to the goals and objectives of the school.

Journaling

Journaling is the process of reflecting and then writing about that reflection. Although a teacher may gather notes and write narratives of what occurred, this activity will not have as great an effect on teaching as journaling will. A teacher new to documenting can begin a teacher journal by taking 5 minutes to think about something significant that happened each day and writing about its significance, how it informs the teacher's knowledge about the child, or the implications for teaching and learning. This focus of thinking could be the class, an individual child, a study such as a project, or the teacher himself and his teaching strategies.

ORGANIZING DISPLAYS OF DOCUMENTATION

When the teacher collects children's work and reflects on it, she often becomes eager to share the knowledge she has gained with others. Many teachers, however, are hesitant about displaying their work. There is much to learn from the Reggio Emilia schools about the importance of display. The displays of the projects done in those schools have traveled the world and convinced many viewers of the importance of their philosophy of education. Edwards and colleagues (1993), in their discussion of the exhibit as a form of communication, identify three key functions of documentation and display:

> [They] provide children with a concrete and visible memory of what they have said and done in order to serve as a jumping off point . . . provide educators with a tool for research and a key to continuous improvement and renewal, and provide parents and the public with detailed information about what happens in the schools as a means of eliciting their reactions and support. (p. 9)

The exhibits of the schools of Reggio Emilia have been successful in fulfilling those functions and can provide to teachers throughout the world encouragement to be brave about sharing the learning that occurs in their own classrooms.

A teacher can begin displaying children's work simply by moving outside the confines of the classroom and into the hallways of the school. According to Loris Malaguzzi (1993), "Throughout the school the walls are used as spaces for both temporary and permanent exhibits of what the children and teachers have created: Our walls speak and document" (p. 57).

However, displays should not be limited to the school environment. Again, the schools of Reggio Emilia have pointed the way. Loris Malaguzzi (1993) tells about first moving displays outside the school.

> I remember that, after a few months, the need to make ourselves known became so strong that we planned a most successful activity. Once a week we would transport the school to town. Literally, we would pack ourselves, the children, and our tools into a truck and we would teach school and show exhibits in the open air, in the square, in public parks, or under the colonnade of the municipal theater. The children were happy. The people saw; they were surprised and they asked questions. (p. 44)

Teachers quickly move from collecting and reflecting to displaying. Displays are eagerly received by parents, administrators, and the community as a whole when they are placed in community locations. Such displays of documentation, with one product done by every child in the class, are much more meaningful than bulletin boards.

A new opportunity for display has become available through the technologies of the Internet and the World Wide Web. The University Primary School at University of Illinois has used their web site to share the documentation of projects that are going on in their classrooms. Nancy Hertzog, the director, meets with the teachers and together they select documentation that Dr. Hertzog then scans into the web site. Parents, children, and other interested individuals can follow the development of projects, viewing children's products, reading project narratives and teacher journals, and seeing photos of children working. A new dimension of interactivity is added by the availability of viewers to respond to the documentation by e-mail to the class.

Matching Displays to Audiences

One of the first things to consider when a teacher is beginning to process his documentation, with the idea of displaying it, is to consider which windows in the framework he wants to open. Is he interested in looking closely at an individual child's development and to sharing that view with others? Is he interested in showing the process of a particular learning experience? Is he interested in focusing on his knowledge and skills as a teacher? The teacher may also want to provide a variety of windows at some time or another from the same set of documentation materials, for example, from a particular project. It is important to think of who will be looking through the window and then plan the display according to the interests of the projected audience.

It is also important for the teacher to revisit the point-of-view experience described in Chapter 3 and to remember that those viewing the display will come with a variety of points of view. Interests, ability to understand, and motivation will vary.

Teachers will often change the location of a display. Selected items may be displayed in the room for children's use, then gravitate to a hallway or public area when the teacher wants to communicate to others what children are learning. Displays in classrooms are often working displays which are evolving and in which children are involved in documenting.

All displays benefit from written descriptions that include the significance of what is displayed, such as what the children have learned, why the item was chosen to be displayed, the process the class used, or what an individual child learned. The description can provide the viewer with an understanding of the educational value of the experiences. Adding to a display, as children's work advances and projects or learning experiences progress increases its value and maintains the interest of observers.

Again, students will benefit from being involved in the display process. Even the youngest children can assist in making a book that tells the story of the project, which can also be used for a display. Older students can evaluate and select the best work for the display and write their own descriptions. As displays are put up or books made, teachers will find it meaningful to provide opportunities for children to reflect on their learning by viewing the displays. When children reflect on their learning experience as they review the documentation, their words can be recorded and added to the narratives accompanying the display. This documentation of the documentation process can provide valuable insight for the teacher in planning additional learning experiences.

It is important for the teacher to plan when and how to share documentation with parents. Parents are significant partners in teaching. Assuming that all parents will see a wall display is probably not realistic. Calling attention to the display, having an open house to view displays, and sharing documentation at parent-teacher conferences are all ways to be sure that parents have an opportunity to experience the joy of watching their children grow and develop. Books about projects, videos, and newsletters can be sent home with children. This is especially helpful for parents who may find it difficult to visit the school.

Principles of Display

When designing a display of documentation, it is important to consider the aesthetic appeal of the exhibit. Teachers in this book were captivated by the care and respect given to the children's work in the Hundred Languages of Children Exhibit. The use of the term *exhibit* is appropriate. It may be helpful for the teacher to visualize exhibiting her children's work in a museum rather than to think about displaying work on a bulletin board. A teacher may wish to visit a museum and observe the way that curators display aesthetic and historical objects. Museum displays provide a good model for teachers in how to display without having the mechanics of the display overwhelm the subject.

Nearly all of the teachers in this book had very little training in displaying children's work. Those with training found that what they had been told about bulletin boards not only did not apply to the goals of displaying documentation but in some cases was contradictory to them. Goldhaver, Smith, and Sortino (1996) also observed that making displays was a challenge to teachers-in-training who were learning to document. Almost all teachers in this book expressed a desire to know how to display their children's work and their documentation in an aesthetically pleasing and productive way.

There are principles of display common to museums that may be helpful for teachers. Eric Douglas articulated ten commandments for museum exhibitors. Some of these commandments are especially applicable to a teacher planning a display.

- have a plan for your exhibit and make it immediately clear to the visitor
- remember that the human eye is lazy and usually looks only ahead and down
- do not allow "eye-catchers" in your exhibits or around them to distract attention from the specimens
- always show objects in their functional position or suggest it to some degree
- always keep your display equipment and mechanics as inconspicuous as possible
- do not arrange monotonous rows of things on shelves or crowd your cases

- compose your displays in three dimensions, using asymmetrical balance as much as possible
- avoid tacking objects flat; hang objects slightly away from the background with the aid of a block
- use labels which approximate the color of the background
- writing should be in large contemporary type and placed below eye level (quoted in Neal, 1976, p. 147)

Many of these recommendations are directly applicable to documentation displays. Having an overall plan for a display can enable the teacher to be sure that viewers will understand the display. A clear starting point for the display is helpful. In the display of projects at several of the schools, the project summary form (see Figure 4.2) was used at the beginning of each display. This form gives the viewer an overview of the project. Framing it in a black mat allows parents and other teachers who regularly view displays identify this summary as the place to start. Another popular form was a handout entitled how to View a Project, which was available for those viewing projects for the first time. This handout explained the purpose of projects, how projects were displayed, how the observer could identify the curriculum goals of the school, and how these goals were integrated into the project.

The most effective displays are those that focus the viewer on the documentation. We feel that teacher-created or commercially created artwork, colorful borders, backgrounds, and posters waste space and time by visually distracting the viewer. Unlike posters for events or print media such as magazines, documentation displays should be designed to encourage the viewer to study the display, not glance at it.

For the same reason, the use of brightly colored or strongly patterned backgrounds is not effective. Walls or backgrounds should complement, not compete with, the work on view (Neal, 1986). It is important that the display be attractive and aesthetically appealing. An eye-catching display can be created through the subtle use of color, texture, and/or pattern. Neal (1986) suggests using varying shades of one basic color to unify a display. Another suggestion is to match the background colors in a display or tablecloth to the content of a display. This also creates viewer interest. For example, softer nature colors complement displays that show children's study of outdoor topics. When exploring background colors, the teacher may find it helpful to examine the predominant colors in the photographs used in the documentation. For example, in the photographs of the Meadow Project, which occurred in the fall, the dominant colors were subtle greens, yellows, and browns. The teacher picked up these colors and enhanced the display by using a dry brush to stroke subtle shades of yellow-green onto the background display material. Burlap and log pieces provided a background for three-dimensional objects (see Figure 9.1). In contrast, the photographs of the bicycle project were mainly taken indoors and featured many pieces of metal, vinyl, and metallic colors. A good choice for the background material for the bicycle display was gray or white.

Narrative, or print, should not overwhelm the display or discourage the viewer from looking. However, a display can appear stark and clinical when it has too much white space, too little text, and a total lack of color. Print must be close to the picture or object for easy identification (see Figure 9.2).

Displays that have more than two dimensions are especially attractive. These can be provided by displaying children's three-dimensional products, such as sculptures or equipment created for play environments. Small shelves can be attached to bulletin boards to provide space if shelving is not available. A spotlight can also be used to highlight an aspect of children's work and to attract attention to the display. Pedestals such as blocks of wood also increase interest in sculpture. Matting, as long as it does not overwhelm, can enhance a drawing or painting. Transparent holders, frames, or pedestals are especially appealing and

Figure 9.1 This display uses three-dimensional items

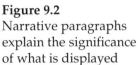

Figure 9.2
Narrative paragraphs explain the significance of what is displayed

take nothing away from the children's work. Use of table mirrors for placement of objects or back mirrors enable viewers to study children's work from more than one direction. This often reveals more of the detail that is indicative of in-depth study and new knowledge and skills.

Creative use of the photocopying machine can focus viewers on children's work. Children's work can be photocopied onto a transparency. It can then be viewed by the whole group of children, or projected onto a wall or shadow screen where children can "get into" their own documentation. The same thing can be done with slides that children or teachers have taken while documenting an experience that they shared together, such as a visit somewhere or a dance or other performance they were involved in. Photocopying can enable the teacher to have additional copies of a document that can be displayed in a variety of ways. In Figure 9.3, photographs of Kendra pretending to be a butterfly were copied. One set was cut out to display a three-dimensional sequence that enabled viewers to understand her expression of movement in a static display.

Using the computer also simplifies and enhances documentation displays. Multiple copies of documentation that apply to more than one child provide a copy for each child's portfolio.

Narratives can be used to enhance wall displays, then reprocessed as a narrative for a children's book to take home. It is possible to make a book for both parents and children, as shown in Part III, "Our Mail Project," by changing the type fonts to differentiate the portions of the narrative intended to be read to the child and those intended to be read by the adult. Use of different fonts or different-colored print will also key viewers into what is most relevant for their purposes when materials are used in displays. Scanning photos of children's work into computer programs holds great promise for documentation.

The computer also often has the added advantage of a spell-checker and grammar-checker. To insure credibility, proper spelling and grammar are important in narratives, captions, and signs shared with the public.

Figure 9.3 The teacher copied photographs and made a 3-dimensional display to show the child's movement

SETTING ASIDE TIME FOR REFLECTING
ABOUT DOCUMENTATION

Documentation cannot inform decision making if it is not thought about, and thinking reflectively is not automatically a part of the teacher's day in many of today's schools. In some schools, thinking about what children are learning occurs only periodically when standardized group achievement tests are given or once a year when state- or district-required assessments are completed. These assessments are not immediately available to the teacher, and teachers are not accustomed to reflecting in depth about children's learning or relating information directly to daily decision making. In addition, in many schools documenting and reflecting on the meaning of the documentation are neither expected of teachers nor reinforced; therefore, they are not a priority in allocation of a teacher's time.

In addition to modeling high-quality documentation, the Reggio Emilia schools have also provided a model for the importance of taking time to reflect on that documentation and to engage in dialogue with colleagues about children's learning. Reflection and engagement of colleagues in discussion deepen the teacher's understanding and can have a significant impact on the growth and development of children.

Setting aside a special time for reflection and journal writing may be the best way to assure that they are given priority. Making a habit of writing in a journal at a regular, specified time, such as the end of each day, can assure that reflection will occur. Sometimes the end of the day is not the best time because the teacher may be tired or have other pressing duties. Other times that teachers have found works for them are during the lunch hour or early the next morning. If it is difficult to set aside a block of time each day for reflection, the teacher can shorten the time by making quick notes of thoughts about the day, documentation gathered, and topics to think about at a later time. Then once a week the teacher can set aside a longer time period to review the short daily notes and write observations.

Sharing with colleagues is an important way to reflect. Loris Malaguzzi (1993) points out the importance of reflecting with colleagues:

> teachers must leave behind an isolated, silent mode of working that leaves no traces. Instead they must discover ways to communicate and document the children's evolving experiences in school. (p. 63)

By designating a portion of staff meetings to share observations and reflections, teachers can set a deadline for themselves. Having to report to someone is often an encouragement to get a task done and to put the extra effort into it in order to meet the deadline. Then, as teachers share their reflections, it is important that others listen and share their insights. It is also helpful to work out an informal agreement with a colleague to meet and discuss reflections. If the teacher has a teacher associate or aide in the classroom, the opportunity to see experiences from two different viewpoints is very valuable. Sharing with colleagues can be on-the-fly, sharing during activities or experiences, at the end of the day, or at a designated time during the day. It is very helpful to set a policy to ask each other daily, "How did we do?" This can become very powerful if the answer is focused on children's learning that has been observed and documented instead of general global feelings of the flow of routine.

Before sharing with colleagues, it is helpful to prepare by gathering together any relevant documentation and deciding on specific events or observations to share. The teacher can determine what kind of input she would like from her colleagues, for example, problem solving, advice on a different way to respond, or ideas for extending a child's experiences. This will focus the discussion and provide a meaningful experience for the teacher. However, everyone should make it a point to be open to other insights or points of view as they emerge while examining the documentation. Keeping a written record of the discussion will provide opportunities for everyone to see the similarity of experiences. Review of the discussion notes at a later time will also document the teacher's growth in dialoguing and observing.

Sometimes it is appropriate to ask a colleague to gather documentation for the teacher by observing or collecting while he is teaching or interacting with children. This can provide rare insight if the teacher tells the colleague what focus he desires. If colleagues are unavailable when an event occurs for which the teacher desires observation and reflection, audio or video recordings can enable joint observation and reflection at a later time.

It is important that reflection with or without colleagues occur on a regular basis, not just at the end of a learning experience. Organizing and reflecting on a regular basis on the photos, notes, and student products provide the basis for adjusting the learning experience, challenging children's thinking, and introducing opportunities for skill development. If reflection is delayed until after a display is assembled or a culminating event occurs, then the experience cannot be altered to achieve maximum growth and development.

Teachers with experience in documenting children's work have found that it is helpful to provide a way to make their documentation readily available for reflection. Tacking documentation on the walls of the classroom or in a staff room, even without explanations or notes, during an experience will help the teacher visualize the process and reflect. Telling others about the significance and the insight provided will elicit additional reflections. These can be used to write more formal summaries and become part of a more public display at a later time.

Another technique that teachers have found to encourage reflection is to regroup different pieces of documentation for making different types of decisions. For example, a documentation of a child learning a skill could become an individual portfolio item but could also be used to show the value of a particular learning experience. As these are used in displays or shared with others, some teachers have found it helpful to make photocopies for multiple use. As the teacher reflects on the documentation, she may color-code her reflections to indicate the viewpoint, or the focus of the reflection. Highlighting and adding borders are other ways to let others know the significance of the documentation.

Organizing and collecting documentation is a long process. It takes commitment by the teacher. If the teacher is sharing the documentation as he "lives it" with his children, he will find that he is able to understand at a greater depth what is occurring in his classroom. As he gains a greater understanding, he will find that he is changing his way of making decisions. In Chapter 10, just what those changes are and how they affect teaching will be examined.

CHAPTER 10

Implementation: Using Documentation for Decision Making

The process of documenting children's learning requires an investment of time and energy by the teacher. The teacher may wonder if this investment is worth the effort, especially if the time spent gathering, processing, and reflecting on experiences means less time spent planning and preparing additional experiences or interacting with parents, colleagues, or the children. It is easy for most teachers to see the value of documenting once they begin to use documentation to inform their teaching or to show others the value of a learning experience.

Showing (or teaching) others about their children and what is happening in their classroom is a familiar task to most teachers. Teachers do this every day, and this task alone is sufficient in impact to justify the time and energy needed for documentation. This is a valid, worthwhile reason to document. The focus of documentation in this instance is outside the teacher; it is another way to communicate with others. However, the greatest value of documentation may be the opportunity that it provides for the teacher to focus inward, on her own skills and knowledge, and in this way it assists the teacher in improving as a professional. Reflection on their own teaching is a recognized and encouraged method for teachers to develop their skills as professionals (Jalongo, 1991; Jones, 1993). The standards for an early childhood/generalist enumerated by the National Board For Professional Teaching Standards (1996) include a focus on reflection. Standard VI requires that "teachers regularly analyze, evaluate, and strengthen the quality of their work."

> For accomplished teachers every class and every activity provides opportunities for reflection and improvement. . . . When they review the work-in-progress and final products of their students, these teachers assess themselves as well as their students. (p. 93)

Reflection on a regular basis is a valid way to grow professionally. Loris Malaguzzi (1993) also affirms the value of self-reflection:

> Teachers must possess a habit of questioning their certainties, a growth of sensitivity, awareness, and availability, the assuming of a critical style of research and continually updated knowledge of children. (p.63)

DECISION MAKING

Teaching is a personal process that is often described as a process of continuous decision making. Examples of decisions that a teacher must make include deciding what kind of environment to provide, how lessons and experiences should be structured, when to move on to a new activity, or how an activity should be modified to meet individual needs. As teachers mature and gain experience, they improve that decision-making process. Documentation supports the teacher in making these decisions by focusing on children's knowledge, skills, and attitudes as she collects and provides evidence for reflecting on the effectiveness of that decision making.

Making a good decision depends on the accuracy, relevance, and reliability of the evidence on which the decision is based. Typically in the past, many decisions, such as when to introduce a concept, were made without analysis or consideration of what the children already knew, what they didn't know, what their disposition was to learn the task, or what else was occurring in the classroom. Timing of the introduction of a topic was often determined by a grade-level guideline that may or may not have been appropriate for a specific child or group of children or by a teacher's arbitrary calendar schedule. If a teacher regularly documents children's work, he knows what skills and knowledge the children have, and he can use that to assist in making a decision about what skill is appropriate to be introduced.

When Beth Crider-Olcott first began to document learning in her classroom for 3- and 4-year-olds, she was teaching sorting as a mathematical thinking skill. She had selected materials that enabled children to sort, she organized circle-time activities in which children sorted together, and she interacted with children in play, such as block play, by calling attention to likenesses and differences and the sorting process. When she began to collect evidence of their sorting skills for their portfolios, she discovered that all the examples she had collected were examples of sorting by one attribute, color. In examining the portfolio items that she had collected, she was also surprised to discover that all of her children already knew how to sort by color.

This evidence had a powerful influence on her decisions for the rest of the year. She made changes in the toys available for children's play by adding toys that involved sorting by shape, size, or use and adding more advanced classifying schema such as farm animals and pets. Activities in circle time focused on sorting items with several attributes instead of only one.

As the variety of opportunities increased for children to do mathematical thinking regarding sorting and classifying, Ms. Crider-Olcott documented how the children responded to the increasing complexity of the tasks. She was able to see the variations in the skill levels of the children. With this information, she then focused on her interaction patterns with individual children. She assisted children who had difficulty sorting according to two attributes by modeling and by talking with them as they thought through the sorting process. She was able to challenge the thinking of children who had mastered sorting according to two attributes by adding additional attributes or adding more complex sorting criteria.

The example of Beth Crider-Olcott and her class's experiences with sorting illustrates how the investment of time and effort in documentation can result in fundamental changes in how the teacher makes decisions. It also shows how these changes are integrated into the classroom and how they result in more effective teaching.

To examine more closely how documentation supports teacher decision making, it is helpful to return to the three windows introduced in Chapter 2—the window on a child's development, the window on a learning experience, and the window for teacher self-reflection.

THE WINDOW ON A CHILD'S DEVELOPMENT

To create a window on a child's development, the teacher uses documentation to examine the individual child's growth and development. This documentation provides insight into the child's knowledge, skills, and dispositions, and serves as a basis for the many important decisions made on a daily and weekly basis. In addition, the teacher often needs to make recommendations regarding placement, referral, or allocation of special resources. Figure 10.1 is a summary of some of the questions asked by the teacher in making decisions about a child's development. The chart also indicates types of documentation that may be useful to the teacher in making these decisions.

As indicated in Figure 10.1, the types of documentation that are most helpful for a teacher in this decision-making process may be those that are individually produced or that focus on individual children. These

Figure 10.1 Types of documentation for the Window on a Child's Development

Decision to be made	Is this child's development on track?	What knowledge and skills need additional instruction?	How does this child learn best?	What are this child's strengths and talents?	Is this child in need of support services or a full evaluation?	Does this family need help to support this child's development?	What are this child's interests?	What dispositions has this child towards school skills?
Type of Documentation								
Narrative for adults			x	x			x	x
Narrative by/for children							x (by)	x (by)
Narrative for display							x	x
Teacher journal		x	x	x	x	x	x	x
Staff dialogue notes		x	x	x	x	x		x
Individualized portfolio items	x	x	x	x	x	x	x	
Core portfolio items	x	x	x	x		x		
Developmental checklists	x	x	x	x	x			x
Verbal language products	x	x	x	x	x	x	x	
Written language products	x	x	x	x	x	x	x	
Pictures	x	x	x	x	x	x	x	
Webs/Lists	x	x	x	x	x	x	x	
Music and movement	x	x	x	x	x	x	x	
Constructions	x	x	x	x	x	x	x	
Statements of disposition			x	x		x	x	x
Reflections on webs		x	x	x			x	x
Tape recordings of self-reflections				x			x	x

include portfolio items such as samples of the child's drawing, writing, constructions, or songs. Anecdotal notes of teacher observations capture skills and knowledge that were demonstrated in the classroom. Developmental checklists on each child are, obviously, extremely valuable in decision making in this window.

Decision Making in Action

Of the various types of documentation indicated in Figure 10.1, children's products provide an especially rich source of information about their development, especially when accompanied by anecdotal notes that describe the process of making that product. Products enable the teacher to make judgments about the quality of the child's work by comparison with products of other children the same age. This is useful for planning lessons and selecting materials and resources. In addition, the teacher develops an understanding of the unique ways in which children approach problems and learn concepts.

In the following example from the Bicycle Project, teacher Jolyn Blank collected Patience and Samuel's work for their portfolio and recorded her observations of how they approached the new task by working through it on their own and how they sorted out their knowledge.

> Today I introduced the bike parts I collected from a local bicycle repair shop. The children got their hands on the parts and studied them carefully. They eagerly began drawing them. Samuel and Patience told Mrs. Boos, "We don't need any help." They then became immersed in their drawing. Patience put extreme care into her drawing of the chain and the chain wheel and then decided to create a second draft. In her second draft, the chain was connected to the chain wheel. Although this was not the case on the parts displayed on the table, she represented how she knew that they were assembled on the bike.

This documentation provided an insight into how Patience liked to work. Ms. Blank realized that Patience liked to figure things out on her own and would carefully work and rework an idea. The next time Ms. Blank made a decision about how to plan a learning experience in which Patience was involved, she added opportunities for Patience to approach learning in this way. The combination of the teacher's anecdotal notes and the product, her drawing, provided this insight.

Many teachers in this book have reported that increasing their documentation enabled them to do a better job of making decisions about whether to introduce new content and skills or reinforce concepts with additional practice. This "teaching to Vygotsky's zone of development," as described in Chaper 1 (Figure 1.3) has enabled them to be more efficient. An example of this is Michelle Didesch's experience with a 4-year-old who was interested in learning to write. Ms. Didesch had been carefully documenting this child's progress in understanding the writing process. She knew that the child understood that writing had a purpose, that writing was done by using letters in a specific order. Ms. Didesch also realized that the child was beginning to understand that there was a relationship between letters and sounds. One day, the child was playing in the housekeeping area, pretending to be a new mother. She came to Ms. Didesch and asked her to make a sign. She wanted it to say "I just had a baby!" Ms. Didesch had a decision to make. She could write the sign for the child; she could write the words for the child to copy; or she could encourage the child to try invented spelling. Her documentation assisted her decision making. Ms. Didesch told the child that she could figure out the letters by listening to the sounds. By slowly saying the words with her teacher, the child wrote, "I jst hd a babe." From that point on the child tried to write with invented spelling.

Had Ms. Didesch not documented this child's progress toward writing, she might have responded by relying on her knowledge of the typical development of 4-year-olds and responded by making a sign for the child. Challenging a child to painstakingly sound out each letter at this age could have been developmentally inappropriate and damaged the disposition to want to write. For many 4-year-olds, who are just learning that there are such things as letters, a model to copy would also have been an age-appropriate response. Because of her documentation, Ms.Didesch was able to make the right decision for that child at that time and encouraged her skill development.

Decisions that inform the teacher about one child's development do not always have to be based on observations or products created by the child alone. A child's participation in a group can also reveal individual knowledge, skills, and dispositions and provide information on the ability of the child to work with others. Parents often provide documentation of what the child does at home, which can also assist the teacher in making decisions about an individual child.

Documentation can lead to much more informed decisions about educating individual children than can individualized information that comes from standardized tests. Information from standardized group-administered achievement tests usually provides a profile of a child's knowledge and skills at a particular point in time. However, because results are not known for some time, the profile is often not up to date or specific enough to inform day-to-day decisions.

THE WINDOW ON A LEARNING EXPERIENCE

As described in Chapter 2, in the discussion of the window on a learning experience, the teacher uses documentation to examine and give others a view of learning processes, such as a project, which involve a group of children. Documentation can show how children's thinking changed; and what concepts, skills, and dispositions were applied and/ or developed through the course of the experience. The teacher can share the impact of the experience with others, such as other children, parents, school administrators, and members of the community. This enables all constituencies to examine the effectiveness of a learning experience. The teacher makes many important decisions before, during, and after each learning experience in which the children are engaged. Figure 10.2 is a summary of some questions frequently asked by teachers and others when making decisions about a learning experience. The chart also indicates types of documentation that would assist the teacher in making these decisions.

As shown in Figure 10.2, some especially helpful types of documentation often come directly from the learning experience. They enable the teacher to direct the experience to maximize the knowledge acquired and the skills developed. Webs completed throughout a project or unit of study assist the teacher in identifying what knowledge children are gaining. The written and verbal language of songs provide insight into growth in both knowledge and skills as well as in vocabulary and the ability to use language to represent learning. An observant teacher can assess children's knowledge when they make and use materials and equipment to construct play environments representing a real place, and when they represent their ideas with blocks, Legos, or sculpture. Additional experiences can then be provided to extend learning. Observation of details and words to describe these details in children's drawings and paintings reveals their growth in knowledge about topics and provides an opportunity for the teacher to see if children are incorporating the vocabulary. Displaying Time 1 and Time 2 versions of the same drawing together provides especially strong evidence of children's learning at the same time that it demonstrates the effectiveness of the experience to stimulate that learning.

The best type of documentation for answering questions about the process of a learning experience, however, may be narratives, those various ways in which children and teachers tell the story of the experience. History boards with photos, books for parents, videos, notes to accompany displays, teacher journals, and project journals are often interesting, thought-provoking, and persuasive. They enable the teacher and children to trace the trail of their learning and see how decisions affect outcomes at various points in the process. Group learning experiences provide unique opportunities for children to learn how to work together. Group interaction skills include how to listen to each other, how to give and receive feedback, and how to cooperate to achieve a common goal. Narratives can provide information about the effectiveness of an experience in developing these skills.

Figure 10.2 Types of documentation for the Window on a Learning Experience

Types of Documentation	Are children engaged in meaningful learning?	Are there opportunities to develop language, literacy, and numeracy?	Are there opportunities to practice thinking skills such as problem solving?	Are children learning how to work together?	Are children learning to use traditional library references?	Are children learning to interview experts, survey, experiment and observe on site?	Are children representing what they know by drawing, writing, building, or discussing?	Are children developing dispositions to question, seek answers and use school skills?
Narrative for adults	X	X	X	X	X	X	X	X
Narrative by/for children	X	X	X	X	X	X	X	X
Narrative for display	X	X	X	X	X	X	X	X
Teacher journal	X	X	X	X	X	X	X	
Staff dialogue notes	X	X	X	X	X	X	X	X
Individualized portfolio items	X	X	X	X	X	X	X	X
Core portfolio items	X	X	X		X	X	X	X
Developmental checklists	X	X	X	X	X	X	X	X
Verbal language products	X	X	X			X		X
Written language products	X	X	X			X	X	
Pictures	X	X	X			X	X	
Webs/Lists	X	X	X			X	X	
Music and movement	X		X				X	
Constructions	X		X	X		X	X	
Statements of disposition	X							X
Reflections on webs	X	X						X
Tape recordings of self-reflections	X							X

Decision Making in Action

An example of how narrative documentation assists the teacher in monitoring the development of group interaction skills is present in this passage, also from the Bicycle Project. It is an excerpt from a narrative written by Suzi Boos and Jolyn Blank describing the progress of their project.

> We have been working on a wall story about bikes. During a small group discussion, Raymond developed the writing structure for a story: "____ likes to ride _____ *(descriptive phrase)*." We began to use our end of the day whole-group meeting as an opportunity to critique the work they had done. We worked on the book over a period of time. A sample of the children's suggestions for improvement is documented here in reference to certain children's work.
>
> WORK: BRITTNEY LIKES TO RIDE IN THE SPRING.
>
> *Justin M:* It's pretty.
> *Justin D:* Good drawing.
> *Teacher:* What do you suggest Brittney could change if she did her page again?
> *Justin D:* Change this to brown. (Justin pointed to a drawing of a puddle colored blue)
> *Ariane:* Yeah, it's a mud puddle.
>
> WORK: SARAH LIKES TO RIDE AND DO WHEELIES.
>
> *Lakeshia:* Sarah is the best drawer. She did a good job on the street and took her time.
> *Justin D:* That's what a street looks like!
> *Ariane:* She needs to put the clouds and the sun in.

This was the children's first experience with doing this. It was a powerful way to involve children in reexamining and reflecting on their work and motivated some of them to revise and increase their own expectations for the quality of their work. This was also the teachers' first experiences with this. We found it very beneficial and will continue to use this technique.

This teachers' narrative provides a window on the learning experience and how it enabled the teachers to see how one strategy, making a wall story, provided an opportunity for children to develop the skills of giving and receiving feedback. The teachers were able to review how the strategy contributed to promoting the group interaction skills they desired. The same piece of documentation also enabled the teachers to reflect on their own decision to incorporate the strategy into the project. This is teacher self-reflection, which is the focus of the next window.

THE WINDOW FOR TEACHER SELF-REFLECTION

In the window for teacher self-reflection, the teacher focuses on his own knowledge and skills and on his role. The teacher uses the documentation to reflect on how his teaching might be strengthened, improved, or modified. Decisions in this area can have a profound effect on children's learning. As the teacher documents and reflects on the documentation, he becomes a better teacher as the results or lack of results of his teaching become visible. If the teacher improves his knowledge and skills while working with one child or one experience, these can carry over from child to child and class to class, affecting many children. Thus documentation, as shown in the web (Figure 3.1) and in Chapters 4-8, has enormous potential for having an impact on education. Decisions in this window are important decisions.

Most types of documentation can be used by the teacher in some way to examine her teaching and improve its quality and effectiveness. An obvious place for a teacher to start would be to look at children's products. The teacher might ask himself, "What are the children producing or not producing?"

Figure 10.3 is a summary of questions teachers can ask themselves about their own development as teachers. It shows what types of documentation may be helpful in answering these questions. This chart differs from the previous two charts, which contained questions that might have been generated by a classroom teacher or parent. The questions in Figure 10.3 were organized around a summary of the eight standards for national board certification as an early childhood/generalist (National Board For Professional Teaching Standards, 1996). The chart can also be used to select and organize documentation for the purpose of providing evidence of professional knowledge, skills, or competencies as delineated by an agency, organization, or supervisor. In this way, documentation can not only assist the teacher in reflecting upon her own professional development but enable her to demonstrate her expertise to others.

Teacher self-reflection as well as reflection about children's work is more beneficial when shared with colleagues. Also included in Standard VI: Reflective Practice of the National Board Certification (National Board For Professional Teaching Standards, 1996) is the requirement that teachers evaluate results and seek input systematically from a variety of sources:

On a regular basis, these teachers seek knowledge and advice from colleagues

Figure 10.3 Types of documentation for the Window on Teacher Self-Relfection

Types of Documentation	Do I understand child development and plan to meet unique needs and potentials?	Do I promote all domains and organize the environment to best facilitate learning?	Do I design and implement appropriate learning experiences within and across disciplines?	Do I use multiple teaching strategies for meaningful learning and social cooperation?	Do I continually monitor and analyze children's activities and behavior to improve teaching?	Do I regularly analyze, evaluate and strengthen the quality and effectiveness of my work?	Do I work with and through parents to support children's learning?	Do I work with colleagues to improve practices for young children and their families?
Narrative for adults		x	x	x		x	x	x
Narrative by/for children		x	x	x				x
Narrative for display		x	x	x		x	x	x
Teacher journal	x	x	x	x	x	x	x	x
Staff dialogue notes	x	x	x	x	x	x	x	x
Individualized portfolio items	x	x		x	x			
Core portfolio items	x	x		x	x			
Developmental checklists	x	x		x	x			
Verbal language products	x	x		x	x			
Written language products	x	x		x	x			
Pictures	x	x		x	x			
Webs/Lists	x	x		x	x			
Music and movement	x	x		x	x			
Constructions	x	x		x	x			
Statements of disposition	x	x		x				
Reflections on webs	x	x		x				
Tape recordings of self-reflections	x	x		x				

through discussions, in-class observations of their own teaching, and personal observation of other teacher's practice. These observations and discussions shape their decisions about if, when, and how their practice should change and create a predisposition to abandon less-effective practices and replace them with most-promising approaches. (p. 93)

Decision Making in Action

In the following two excerpts from Dot Shuler's diary of the project they did on rocks in her second-grade class, you can see how Ms. Shuler followed the progress of her class toward the goal "using references to gain information" and then "using information in representations."

> While silent reading this morning, Troy also found a hardness scale of sorts. It showed talc on one end and a diamond on the other. They're beginning to discover the information without my telling them a thing. I am so proud of them!

> From the journals that were read aloud today, we had a story about the softness of talc, one about the three kinds of rocks, and one about the layers of the earth—all of them were the result of silent reading. They are discovering on their own!

In the next passage, her diary shows how she had been evaluating the quality of the work they were producing and had concerns about it. She felt that they did not understand the importance of quality, so in response she opened a discussion of the problem.

> One day this week, we stopped for a class discussion on the quality of work and its importance in representations like graphs. I just discussed it, with concern and interest. They said they understood, and upon going back to centers, two asked me if they could do their graph over.

The result of her calling attention to her goals resulted in children's redoing their work voluntarily. When deciding what to do in future experiences, Ms. Shuler will most likely alter her instructions to address this issue before work begins.

Mary Jane Elliott shares the following reflection on her teaching. It is a narrative of a conversation that she had with her students after she showed them a documentation board on the "Apple" project that they did in her kindergarten. She had prepared the display for presentation to a professional audience.

Erica raised her hand and said, "You know, Mrs. Elliott, that all of those ideas on the board were the children's. We did the investigations, and those were our words you typed and put on the board. The only thing you did was go around and take pictures!" This was the best compliment I have ever received about my teaching. Indeed, the work on the board was the project work designed and directed by the children themselves. I was a co-learner and a facilitator. That one of my children actually recognized my role for what it was still astounds me!

After this reflection, it is very likely that Ms. Elliott will again decide to put her children in charge of their own learning.

Both of the previous examples of documentation supporting teacher self-reflection resulted in insight into the effectiveness of teaching strategies and benefited these teachers and the children in their care. Other teachers also gained from these insights through discussions in which they vicariously experienced the decisions made. Another way that teacher reflections can be shared with other teachers and administrators is through history books and displays. All of these methods of sharing documentation help others to see the teacher as a learner who is growing professionally and encourage colleagues to reflect on their own teaching.

MAKING REFLECTION A PRIORITY

A critical element in the use of documentation for decision making is time to reflect. In Chapter 9 there are ideas for teachers of how this can be accomplished in the section "Setting Aside Time for Reflecting About Documentation." Time is needed to reflect on the documentation and to organize displays; teachers also need time to discuss with and provide input to one another.

Time, however, is not always controlled by the teacher. Administrators who schedule planning and preparation periods so that teachers can meet together and who provide materials and space for documentation encourage teachers to document. These administrators are likely to be rewarded by improved quality of decision making in their programs and greater progress toward meeting their goals for children and families.

CHAPTER 11

Documentation As Assessment: Building Credibility

credibility: —1. The quality, capability, or power to elicit belief.
—*American Heritage Dictionary*, (1994)

In the previous chapters we have seen how documentation provides three windows for viewing the educational process, how the teacher can create those views, and how they can have an impact on and improve teaching. "What happened in school today?" is the question that Lilian Katz raises in the Foreword to this book. She reminds us that the school and the relationship of the school and parent are only part of the reasons for documentation, there is also the perception of the outside world of early childhood education.

It may be helpful for readers to create an image of a school with three windows and then imagine themselves backing off and looking at the school from afar. In this image, the school is surrounded by other buildings, other institutions, and a city with diverse people with diverse needs and beliefs. Children, staff, and families who enter and exit the school with many different points of view and those outside who are not part of the process also have a variety of expectations and points of view. At this time, the world outside that school is in a turmoil of discussion and debate about school reform, assessment, national standards, and statewide testing. For this reason, it is important that the process of documentation have credibility; that is, that those people, who, for whatever reason, come to view children's work have confidence that what they are seeing is indicative of what is happening to children's growth and development; that information is being gathered in a systematic, reliable way; that children are getting equal opportunities to demonstrate their knowledge and skills; and that the interpretations being made are valid. The early childhood teacher must have a firm grasp of the complexity of assessment and evaluation both to make sure that the documentation process informs her own teaching and to be able to converse with others with different points of view in a knowledgeable way.

ASSESSMENT

How does the term *assessment* relate to documentation, as described in this book? Assessment is defined by the National Association for the Education of Young Children (Bredekamp & Rosegrant, 1995) as

> the process of observing, recording and otherwise documenting the work children do and how they do it, as a basis for a variety of educational decisions that affect the child, including planning for groups and individual children and communication with parents. (p. 11)

Performance assessment, another term used frequently, refers to a type of educational assessment in which the judgments made are based on a child's performance, such as behavior or products (Stiggins, 1994). *Authentic assessment* is another term often heard today.

> Assessment is authentic when we directly examine student performance on worthy intellectual tasks. Traditional assessment, by contrast, relies on indirect or proxy "items"—efficient simplistic substitutes from which we think valid inferences can be made about the student's performance at those valued challenges. (Wiggins, 1990, p. 1)

All of these terms and their definitions apply to the types of documentation in this book. However, it is possible that many early childhood teachers would not recognize or speak about the documentation that they do in their classrooms as assessment. Tynette Hills (1992) points out that when early childhood teachers are asked what they associate with assessment, they list such things as testing, screening, observation, records, and report cards.

> Distressingly often, they speak of assessment methods that are incongruent with the goals and objectives of their programs. Sometimes kindergarten and primary teachers sound as if they are reading from an atlas—Iowa, California, Metropolitan! as they cite or indict group standardized achievement tests. (p. 44)

One of the goals of this book is to open teachers' eyes to additional opportunities for assessing and give them the confidence to use observations and children's work as evidence of children's learning.

GUIDELINES FOR THE ASSESSMENT PROCESS

There are many reasons to assess, and it is important to remember to identify the purpose of assessment when discussing assessment issues.

Hills (1992) describes assessment as formal or informal, with formal assessment relying on readiness, developmental screening tests, criterion–referenced achievements tests, and developmental assessment tests that have high reliability and validity. She describes observation, parent reports, error analysis of children's work, structured observations, teacher–made tests, and analysis of work samples as informal types of assessment. She concludes:

> Informal types of assessment, done systematically and well, can serve all purposes except the purpose of identifying and diagnosing children with special needs. . . . In fact, informal methods should be the primary form of assessment in early childhood programs to assure that teaching and assessing are complementary and developmentally appropriate approaches are employed. (pp. 48–49)

The National Association for the Education of Young Children has assembled guidelines for appropriate assessment for planning instruction and communicating with parents and also for program evaluation (see Bredekamp & Rosegrant, 1995). These guidelines are a valuable way to think about the types of documentation presented in this book. They point out the advantages to the types of documentation used by the teachers whose samples are shared. Within these guidelines are also some cautions for the teachers as they document. We want to highlight six of the guidelines.

Guideline 5 recommends that assessment involve "regular and periodic observation of the child in a wide variety of circumstances that are representative of the child's behavior in the program over time" (Bredekamp & Rosegrant, 1992, p. 23). This guideline is a good reminder that observations and information gathered are more beneficial if they are collected regularly and periodically (over a specific period of time). Collecting information only when a project is going on will provide a window on the learning experience but will not provide enough data to evaluate a child's ongoing development or cover all areas.

Guideline 8 reminds teachers to use an array of types of documentation and not to focus on just one way of documenting. Guideline 15 emphasizes the importance of sharing documentation with children so they can learn to self–evaluate.

Guideline 16, recommends that assessment indicate both "what children can do independently and what they can demonstrate with assistance, because the latter shows the direction of their growth" (p. 17). This guideline emphasizes the importance of collecting children's work even when the child is working with another child or is being assisted by the teacher. As shown in the examples provided in this book, it is important to indicate in an anecdotal note or narrative accompanying a product whether assistance did occur. One area of learning where this indication is particularly significant is in assessing writing. A child may make a sign to label a construction which he created. To use the sign as evidence of the child's skills in writing, it is critical that the teacher note whether the sign was copied from a teacher model, whether the teacher helped the child by saying the words slowly and the child chose the appropriate letter, or whether the child wrote the sign independently. The value of carefully dating and writing down the context from which the sample emerged cannot be overemphasized.

Guidelines 17 and 18 emphasize the importance of systematically setting aside time to reflect on the child's development, to analyze the information, and to share it with parents and colleagues.

THE PROBLEM OF RELIABILITY

One of the reasons documentation might not have the credibility the teacher might want is that others may question reliability and bias. These are common concerns with all types of assessment. When a teacher relies on less formal or constraining assessment strategies, she will want to plan carefully so that her assessment program will assure objectivity and accountability (Gullo, 1994).

In many of the schools from which examples in this book were collected, there was a comprehensive, performance–based assessment system in place. Checklists were completed at regular intervals, children's work was collected in a systematic way, and there was a planned system for review of the observational data and the children's work. Documentation from projects or other learning experiences provided rich, informative work samples and observational notes that were then incorporated into those processes. Two of the schools used the Work Sampling System, which uses a developmental checklist based on national curriculum guidelines and child development research, and a Core Item system that requires that the same type of work be collected from each child three times a year in five domains of learning. Research on this system has shown that it provides teachers with reliable and valid data about children's school performance (Meisels, Liaw, Dorfman, & Fails, 1993). A number of other developmental checklists also have data on reliability; it can be found in the manuals accompanying the checklists.

Even though reliability and validity data are adequate in the Work Sampling System, two of the schools are involved in a training program to increase the reliability of teacher judgments through the development of guidelines and expectations at the beginning of the year, at the middle of the year, and at the end of the year for each Core Item. For example, after teachers have collected Core Item 1 for Language and Literacy (a sample of a child's writing), they gather together to review research on children's writing, to sort and re–sort children's samples in order to develop a sense of typical development of this Core Item for each age level, and to write guidelines or expectations for each age level through the year. This process will increase the probability that judgments based on this Core Item are similar to the judgments that would be made by another teacher and that they are in agreement with expectations suggested by national professional groups and state objectives.

This process will also serve as a professional development opportunity for teachers. Teachers whose projects have been shared in this book often spoke of the need for more information on typical development, or what should be expected. If there is no scheme in the teacher's mind of the typical development of a skill such as writing, or what a particular sample might indicate about a child's development along a continuum of skill development, the advantages of documenting for informing teaching are greatly reduced. As a teacher documents, he can sharpen his knowledge about typical development by carefully comparing, contrasting, and discussing with colleagues, as described in Chapter 10. Carefully documenting the learning that is occurring in their own classrooms is an excellent way for teachers to expand and solidify their knowledge. Many states are involved in efforts to establish guidelines or rubrics for portfolio assessment and to train teachers in their use. Bowers, (1995) reveiws the success and conclusions of those efforts.

THE PROBLEM OF BIAS

When using informal methods of assessment, it is important to avoid bias and address the issue of equity and fairness. Bias is defined as "any attitude, belief, or feeling that results in, and helps to justify, unfair treatment of an individual because of his or her identity" (Derman-Sparks, 1989, p. 3). Teacher bias can result in inaccurate observations or faulty interpretations of data. According to Cohen, Stern, and Balaban (1997),

> Teachers often have feelings about children whose ethnic, racial, or cultural group differs from their own. Negative or fearful reactions to children in wheelchairs, to children who cannot see or hear, or to children with other disabilities such as those resulting from Down syndrome, cerebral palsy, autism, or spina bifida may arise in teachers. Disapproving opinions about gays and lesbians are sometimes projected on children or children's parents.

Teachers may ascribe particular behaviors as acceptable for boys but unacceptable for girls. Bias is at work when a teacher describes an inquisitive boy as "bright" and an inquisitive girl as a "chatterbox." (p.4)

Bias in assessment can have devastating consequences because it affects teacher decision making. Yet, according to Lynch and Hanson (1992), "Cultural bias is often most evident in the assessment process" (p. 362).

One way teachers can be biased is through embeddedness in their own culture. Lynch and Hanson (1992) urge that anyone working with children and families strive to develop cross–cultural competence, a way of thinking and behaving that enables members of one cultural, ethnic, or linguistic group to work effectively with members of another. They recommend that professionals develop competence in three ways:

1. By developing self–awareness, an understanding and appreciation of their own culture and how that culture has affected how they think and behave.
2. By developing culture–specific awareness and understanding of children and families with whom they work through reading, talking with members of the cultures, and sharing daily lives.
3. By learning about cross–cultural communication, the differences between cultures of both verbal and nonverbal communication.

Bias can also result from children's not having an equal opportunity to demonstrate a skill or knowledge. This inequality can come from prior knowledge and experiences, cultural experiences, language proficiency, cognitive style, or interests (Lam, 1995). In the types of documentation discussed in this book, assessment can occur in a variety of ways to meet a variety of individual needs in such a way that bias should be reduced. Children are assessed as they are engaged in active, meaningful learning that has relevance to them and their lives. It is possible, however, for teachers not to look for a variety of ways that a child might demonstrate knowledge, for example, by focusing only on one type of documentation, such as language products. In this case, the teacher will need to try other methods of documenting the child's knowledge. The teacher needs to be cautious in concluding that because she has not documented a skill for a specific child, that it isn't there. An undocumented skill or area of knowledge should be a warning to the teacher to try another way to document, since the child may not have had an opportunity to reveal a skill or knowledge. The teacher needs to guard against thinking that a child's development in one area, such as verbal fluency, means that he is equally advanced in all other areas, such as mathematics, when this may not be the case. Systematically observing and collecting children's work from each learning area or domain throughout the year can assure that the teacher will look at the whole child and each skill area independently.

Bias can also occur if a child has not been asked or chosen to participate in a project or learning experience: Engaged problem solving cannot be observed when the child has not had an opportunity to demonstrate it. All children at the early childhood level do not need to be involved in all projects or learning experiences in a classroom. All children, however, at some time during the year, need the opportunity to do so and to have their approach to learning thoroughly documented.

Avoiding bias in the assessment process requires teacher commitment and effort. Open collegial relationships in which teachers can reflect together on the documentation can also assist in avoiding bias. It is often easier for someone else to see how bias can have an impact on our decision making.

CONCLUSION: TEACHING WITH INTEGRITY

Learning how to document children's work has been a successful and fulfilling experience for many of the teachers in this book. Extensive documentation of children's work has enabled them to meet some of the challenges discussed in Chapter 1. Perhaps the most powerful effect of documentation is that children gain satisfaction from their own efforts and see the appreciation of those efforts by parents and other adults who are important in their lives. Teachers who document have observed that as they increased the attention given to documentation, children have become more careful about their work and more evaluative. For example, we have seen that documenting children's first, second, and even third attempts at a task such as drawing and labeling a vegetable has resulted in children's talking about the growth that has occurred. The time and effort that teachers devote to gathering information on children's work has communicated clearly to the children that what they are doing is important. Even the youngest children have come to understand the excitement that evidence of their learning can generate in their parents.

Teacher Judy Cagle documented a 4-year-old's writing about his mother's reaction to the documentation of a project on reflections that was displayed in the hallway. Perhaps copying the writing that he had seen his teacher do when making anecdotal notes, Dion wrote a series of letterlike shapes that the teacher then collected as a writing sample for documenting growth in language and literacy. Mrs. Cagle had written the following note and dictation on the sheet on which she mounted his story.

> Dion used letters and letterlike forms to write about his mother's visit to the class to see the Reflections Project. His writing says, "My mom saw reflections in the hallway. Her said, 'Wow!'"

Any careful systematic documentation requires teacher commitment and effort. Many teachers may hesitate to step in and try it. However, it is important to remember our image of the school and our view from afar. We can see that there are many challenges to both the school and the community that surrounds it. These challenges are not likely to go away quickly. Documentation as described in this book can help meet those challenges.

One of the ways we can help people understand the value of early childhood education and what schools do is to throw open the windows and invite people to look. We may have reached the point where, in the words of Loris Malaguzzi, "the need to make ourselves known became so strong" (Edwards, et al., 1993) that we, like the teachers in Reggio Emilia, need to make the effort to document our children's work.

As we were completing this book, some of the teachers whose work is in the book were discussing Steven Carter's (1996) definition of integrity. He divides it in to three parts:

(1) discerning what is right and what is wrong;
(2) acting on what you have discerned, even at personal cost; and
(3) saying openly that you are acting on your understanding of right and wrong. (p. 7)

It occurred to many of the teachers that how we assess children, how we make decisions about their education, and how we present early childhood education to the public have become issues of integrity, issues of what is right and wrong with significant consequences for children and families. These teachers thought about the right thing to do when assessing and teaching children, they found a way to capture the active, engaged learning occurring in their classroom, and now they are sharing it with the readers of this book.

The success of their documentation to inform their teaching and communicate with others can be seen from the many examples in this book. It was worth the investment of time and energy. However, a side effect, not predicted but perhaps the most far-reaching, was the frequently reported increase that teachers experienced in their joy in teaching and the parents' joy in their children's learning.

PART III

An Example of Documentation

"Our Mail Project" Memory Book

A Narrative Documentation

The following pages were originally a memory book entitled **Our Mail Project** which I made to share with "audiences" who could not come to our school and see our project displays. My goal was to share with a diverse audience, including both adults and children, knowledge about what the children learned during the project and early childhood principles that corresponded with that learning. I wanted my students' families and others to know what and how my students learn while they are in school.

The original book was formatted similarly to the pages that follow. It had three different formats of text. Each format used a different font and writing style. The first format consisted of photographs accompanied by a narrative written in large bold type and simple text. This served as a history of our project that could be shared with children. The second format included principles of early childhood in which I strongly believe. I supported each principle with evidence from our project experience. The principles are printed in bold type separated from the supportive evidence so that the reader can easily find them. In addition, the principles are printed on blue paper. The third format included some of my personal struggles and reflections. I wanted the readers, especially my colleagues, to know that I also learned from our project experience. My reflections appear on pink pages in the original book with a descriptive heading at the top of the pages. Colored paper, different sizes of type, and bold type drew the reader's attention to the variety of points of view.

In constructing the book, I used page protectors and a three ring binder. I wanted the pages to be protected while the book was being circulated from home to home. In addition, the binder gave me the freedom to rearrange the pages or remove pages.

Writing and constructing the book took some time. However, the knowledge that I was able to share with so many people including children, parents, grandparents, teachers, and administrators was well worth the effort. I strongly recommend this form of documentation.

Our Mail Project

An In-depth Study

by
The Students and Teachers of Yellow 2

Adam	Curtisia	Matthew
Amber	Dominique	Michael
Andy	John	Ryan
Anthony	Joni	Timothy
Brian	Karissa	Timothy
Brittany	Kayla	Tres

Kathy Steinheimer   Tammy Shinkey

AN INTRODUCTION FROM THE TEACHER

In the middle of *A Letter to Amy* by Ezra Jack Keats (1968), the main character of the book, Peter, places an invitation in a city mailbox. The next time the invitation is seen in the story Amy, Peter's friend, is taking it out of her mailbox. After listening to this story several times, my class, Yellow 2, a class of eight 3-year-olds and ten 4-year-olds, was curious as to what happened to the letter between the points where Peter mailed the invitation and Amy received it. My students' interest in this process led me to consider mail as a possible project topic, and I planned a classroom meeting to survey my student's knowledge of the topic.

During our class meeting, I asked my students to discuss how a letter gets from one place to another. I wrote down their comments in the form of a flow chart. Afterwards, I reflected on this initial discussion and documentation. I concluded that my students' knowledge of the mail process was limited, and their interest in learning more was high. Every child had actively engaged in the discussion either as a speaker and/or listener. My students had already invested in the topic. I then decided that the mail system would be our project topic and began planning accordingly. During this initial planning stage, I set six goals for our project. First, I wanted each member of my class to have some responsibility in making decisions concerning the direction of our project. Secondly, I wanted to provide opportunities for my students to grow in their ability to work as a team. Thirdly, I wanted my class to be able to provide a service for their school. Fourth, I wanted my students to begin to understand how to investigate and research a topic. Fifth, I set a goal that involved providing ample opportunities to enhance my students' abilities to solve problems. Finally, I wanted my students to learn how to reflect on what they were learning as they documented and shared it with others. I wanted my students to become experts on the topic of mail.

I set these goals while visualizing the mail project as a catalyst for helping my students work with their "growing edges." I also realized that the path we would travel from point A (limited knowledge of our topic) to point B (sophisticated knowledge of our topic) was not going to be a straight line. In fact, I knew that the children and I would gain so much more if I allowed us to take a meandering path from point A to point B. Thus, I reviewed my project goals and began to plan a pathway for our project that was flexible and allowed for the creativity and insight of my students.

During this initial planning stage, I saw our project as having three components. I wanted to develop a pen pal system for our school, which would create a large volume of mail and therefore a need for a mail system. My students would be challenged to meet that need as they worked to develop and manage a mail system. The second component would involve the study of real objects. I wanted to use collections of stamps and envelopes to enhance my students' ability to investigate, research, and organize what they had learned. Finally, I wanted our project to include a component that would give my students many opportunities to document and reflect on their own work and the work of others. I knew that this documentation would take many forms; however, I did not know exactly what types of documentation my students would use.

At this point, I must stress that my planning was general. I considered the direction of our project, not the detail. The detail of a project must be done in partnership with the children. It is important for children to play an active role in all phases of a project including planning or they will not take ownership of the project. I told my students about my decision to make mail a project topic and shared my ideas with them soon after our initial flow chart discussion. My students were eager to get started, and we entered the next phase of our project.

My students developed and operated the mail system for our school during this phase which lasted approximately 4 weeks. This mail system included making and selling stamps, mail pick-up, sorting, and delivery. This required several constructions including mailboxes, mailbags, and a mail truck. In addition, this phase gave my students and me ample opportunities to document and reflect on our learning. During this phase, I began to document our learning in a project journal. This journal helped me reflect on our progress and formalize my next step based on what the children were learning. As I wrote each night in my journal, I was amazed by the variety and extent of my students' growth. We were meeting my project goals and more.

The operating of the mail system naturally led to a study of several collections of real objects. For example, when my students researched mailboxes to see how to make them for individual classrooms, they began to talk about their own mailboxes. A study on mailboxes was launched. In the same way, using canceled stamps as postage for their pen pal letters led to a study of stamps. We used a variety of envelopes for mailing our letters and later began a study of envelopes. The study component of our mail project lasted approximately 2 weeks and provided many opportunities for growth in the ability to collect and analyze data, reflect on learning, and share learning with others. In addition, I made sure that my students had many opportunities to work cooperatively with each other.   My students began their final reports of the various aspects of the mail project during the fifth and sixth weeks of the project. The children documented their own work by making several large classroom books that described and showed how the mailboxes, mailbags, and mail truck were made. These books consisted of a series of photographs and a brief dictation that described the construction process. The dictation was either copied onto the pages by myself or students. The photographs were then taped by the students to the appropriate pages. They also used photographs to create a book about post office functions such as sales and mail sorting. In addition, my students created a book that described and illustrated the mail process using our final flowchart as reference. All of these books helped the children organize and reflect on what they had learned.   Finally, the children wanted to share their mail books, constructions, and post office set-up with others. They invited our pen pals over for an open house. Each of my students presented a different aspect of our project to our visitors. As documentation displays appeared and expanded on the walls inside and outside our classroom, many visitors commented on how much the children knew and how well they presented their information. My class had become experts on the topic of mail.

In addition to growing tremendously in knowledge, my students grew in several other areas. Each of my students grew substantially in their ability to work with their "growing edges." It would take a long time to list the skills that my students gained from this experience. This memory book will provide the reader with many examples of how children grow in skills and abilities during a project. My students are now confident in their ability to study a subject in-depth and have the disposition to do so. I am convinced that the project was the reason for their tremendous growth.

In conclusion, I recommend that the reader carefully study our mail memory book, especially the photographic documentation. It is my hope that our project scrapbook will help the reader see that any group of young children can conduct an in-depth study using the project approach. For if we dare to let them, our young children, even 3-year-olds, will show us how capable they really are.

Our Flowcharts

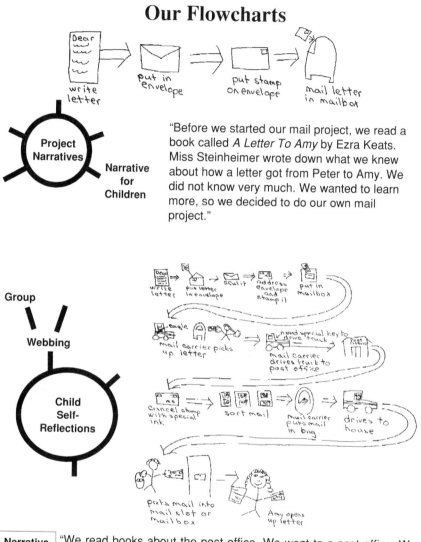

"Before we started our mail project, we read a book called *A Letter To Amy* by Ezra Keats. Miss Steinheimer wrote down what we knew about how a letter got from Peter to Amy. We did not know very much. We wanted to learn more, so we decided to do our own mail project."

| Narrative for Children | "We read books about the post office. We went to a post office. We wrote to our pen pals. And, we organized and operated our own post office for our school. Then, Miss Steinheimer wrote down what we |

had learned. We filled a whole page with pictures and words about how a letter gets from one person to another. We learned a lot! Later, we made our chart into a book. Some of us drew mail trucks, postal workers, mailboxes, and a post office. Several of us learned how to make our own envelopes. We also learned how to use a gluestick to glue the pictures onto the pages. We told Miss Steinheimer what to write on each page."

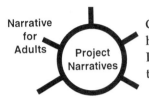

Narrative for Adults — Project Narratives

Creating flow charts with young children helps them understand a sequence of events. Revisiting a flow chart helps children see their own gains in knowledge.

The first flow chart was created after the children had listened to the book *A Letter To Amy* (Keats, 1968) several times. It shows a beginning and limited understanding of the mail system. The second flow chart was created 4 weeks into their mail project. The children told me what to draw, when to draw it, and what words to add to the pictures. This growth in knowledge about the mail system is from active involvement in the in-depth study. Activities included receiving mail, writing to pen pals, organizing and operating a mail system for their school, and constructing items needed for that system. The last flow chart, made in the form of a classroom book, was created by the children during the sixth and final week of the project and was the children's final report.

A 4-year-old's mail truck drawing   A 3-year-old's mail truck drawing

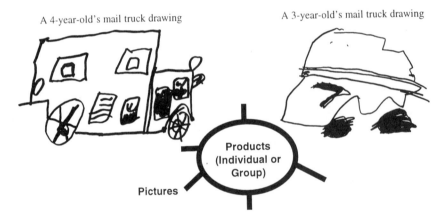

Products (Individual or Group)

Pictures

Narrative for Adults

When young children are given opportunities to observe real objects, they will produce more detailed drawings than if they only have second hand experiences with objects.

These drawings of mail trucks were created by a 4-year-old and a 3-year-old after they explored two different mail trucks at two different times, looked at pictures of mail trucks in books, and created a mail truck for their own postal system. Each child incorporated details into their drawings such as the stripes on the truck or headlights. These drawings are some of the first drawings of vehicles that these two children created. The drawings became part of the children's final flow chart book.

Our Pen Pals

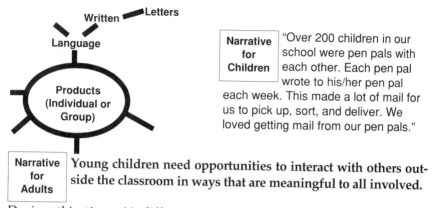

| Narrative for Children | "Over 200 children in our school were pen pals with each other. Each pen pal |
wrote to his/her pen pal each week. This made a lot of mail for us to pick up, sort, and deliver. We loved getting mail from our pen pals."

| Narrative for Adults | **Young children need opportunities to interact with others outside the classroom in ways that are meaningful to all involved.** |

During this time, 14 different classrooms participated in a pen pal experience. This created a need for a postal system. The children of Yellow 2 met that need by organizing and operating a mail system for their school for 3 weeks. This mail system included stamp production and sales, mail pick up once a week, sorting, and delivery of the mail once a week. In addition, the children of Yellow 2 were pen pals with the children of Green 1. All of these experiences enhanced the children's knowledge of their school and the people in it. Other students and adults in the building also interacted with each other through the pen pal system. Approximately 200 people benefited from this project. The children of Yellow 2 had an impact on their world.

| Narrative for Adults | **CONCEPT OF A LETTER.** The children were first introduced to the concept of a letter when they listened to the story entitled *A Letter To Amy* by Ezra Keats (1968). This book |
provided limited information about what a letter was and how a person would write one. It did not provide details, such as the need for an addressed envelope. As the project progressed, we built on this beginning knowledge by using books about mail, receiving letters from people who work at our school, and corresponding with our own pen pals within the building. By the end of the project, the children's knowledge about letters increased. For example, many knew how to "sign" a letter at the end, fold it so that the letter would fit in an envelope, seal the envelope, place a stamp in the appropriate place, and address the envelope. They also added several words to their vocabulary such as stamp, seal, sign, address, stationery, and envelope.

Our Mailboxes

Narrative for Children	"Karissa, Matthew, Tim, and Amber recorded the village color and room number for each room in our school. Then they counted how many rooms they had recorded on their lists. They said that we would need 20 mail boxes."

Narrative for Adults	**Young children need opportunities to gather and analyze data meaningful to them.**

Two teams of two children each were given the task of recording the village color and number for each room in the school. To accomplish this task, the children had to decide such things as who would carry the clipboard and who would record the village color and number for each room. One team argued about who would carry the clipboard throughout two villages. In addition, using a recording process was new to all of them. However, after the first two villages, the children felt capable of recording a village without their teacher. They used the data to find the total number of mailboxes needed and to create an address that consisted of a village color letter and number for each room. Thus, their data collection was purposeful and useful to many others.

| Narrative for Children | "Each room needed an address. They gave each room a letter for the room's village color and a number. The address for our classroom was Y2. Y is the first letter in our village color, and 2 is our room number." |

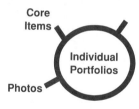

Core Items

Individual Portfolios

Photos

This experience produced a Mathematical Thinking Core Item for each team member.

| Narrative for Adults | **MATHEMATICAL PROBLEM SOLVING.** After the two teams collected their data, I had the children regroup. I asked, "How many mailboxes will you need?" The children |

looked at their charts and counted each room listed for one village. They said that they would need five mailboxes. I pointed out that five mailboxes would only cover one village since each village consists of five classrooms. Then, Tim counted the rooms on the two data sheets and said that they would need ten and ten mailboxes. I asked, " Do you need ten mailboxes?" He said, "Yeah." However, Amber got busy and counted all of the rooms listed and came up with twenty-one mailboxes. I asked Tim to double check her work. He correctly stated that they needed twenty mailboxes. All agreed and recorded this number for the mailbox painting crew.

| Narrative for Children | "Some of us painted lots of cardboard boxes for mailboxes. They used many different colors. Some of us counted the mailboxes to make sure that we had enough for the whole school. We needed 20 mailboxes all together." |

Narrative for Children | "After the paint dried on the boxes, some of us put the addresses on the mailboxes. Some of us cut the paper. Some of us wrote down the addresses. And some of us taped the addresses onto the boxes. It was a big job! We had to work together to get it done. When all of the mailboxes were ready, some of us took them to the classrooms. The children needed them to drop their pen pal letters into for postal pick up."

Teacher

Project Narratives

The paragraph below is based on an entry from the teacher's project journal.

Narrative for Adults | **INDEPENDENCE AND RISK TAKING BY THE TEACHER AND THE CHILDREN.** When the time came to deliver the mailboxes, I grouped the children into pairs and had them deliver the mailboxes on their own. I tried to pair a "veteran" child with a "rookie" in hopes that they would return "safely." Most pairs did very well. However, one pair could not find their destination and had to come back. They set out again with another child more knowledgeable about the layout of the school. Another pair, who were supposed to go to the Green Village, headed for the opposite end of the building. However, they turned around after I suggested that they read the address on their mailbox. During the completion of this task, the children showed their ability to navigate their school and work independently of the teacher. The experience was rewarding for all of us.

Our Post Office

Captions
& Signs

|

Written

Language

Products
(Individual or
Group)

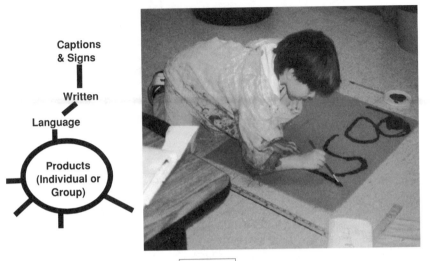

Narrative for Children	"Tim painted the sign saying 'Post Office.'"

Narrative for Adults	Young children need opportunities to count objects for a specific

meaningful purpose. Thus, they internalize the importance of this skill and have several opportunities to practice counting.

The children counted envelopes and placed them in groups of 10 in preparation for the morning's envelope sales at their post office.

In the making of the stamps for their postal system, the children cut the stamps into strips of 5 and 10 stamps, placing them into the appropriate compartment. Both of these activities involved repetitive counting.

Narrative for Children	"Some of us counted envelopes and put them into piles of 10. We sold 10 envelopes for 10 cents. Some

of us made postage stamps to sell at our post office. They wrote a 1 on each stamp because each stamp cost 1 cent."

| Narrative for Children | "On Mondays we sold stamps and envelopes to children from all over our school. We learned how to wait on customers. We learned how to ask, |

'May I help you?' And we learned how to say 'Thank you.' We also counted stamps, envelopes, and real money."

| Narrative for Adults | **Children need opportunities to practice social skills in context.** |

While selling stamps and envelopes at their post office, the children were given opportunities to practice many social skills that are involved in waiting on customers such as asking "May I help you?" In addition, the customers were required to state clearly what they needed, which is sometimes a difficult task for young children. All of the children had some difficulty with these skills at first. However, with practice, they

| Narrative for Adults | **SIDELIGHTS.** Working at the post office introduced the children to much more than working with customers. For example, John learned how to open up a paper sack. Anthony |

inquired about the different types of coins. And Amber discovered a wheat penny. Our project was filled with many of these "learning surprises" that evolved from the children's own curiosity and interest.

Individualized Items

The experience described above resulted in several Individualized Items for the children's portfolios.

Individual Portfolios

Our Sorting Process

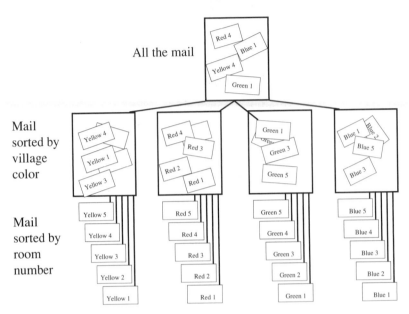

| Narrative for Children | "First, we made a plan for sorting the mail. Miss Steinheimer made a chart of our plan." |

| Narrative for Adults | **Children will re-create or re-enact activities that are meaningful to them. This re-creation enhances their understanding of a subject.** |

A chart used to explain the initial mail sorting process was created by me with the help of the children. The chart was then displayed in the classroom. Several children were observed studying the chart at various times. Several also re-created the chart on their own initiative, demonstrating the importance of the chart to them. In addition, the children demonstrated their understanding of the mail sorting process when they described the charts that they made.

| **Narrative for Children** | "On Tuesdays, some of us picked up the mail from each room." |

| **Narrative for Children** | "On Wednesday, we sorted the mail. First, Kayla took a letter out of the box and gave it to the stamp cancelers. The stamp cancelers canceled the stamps, so that we knew that the stamps had been used." |

| Narrative for Children | "Next, the readers read the address and put a color dot on the envelope. The dot was the same color as the village color. Then, the letters were put into the village box that matched the color dot." |

| Narrative for Adults | **Young children can gain from participating in experiences that require teamwork.** |

In the first sorting of the mail, I assigned each child a specific job. For example, several young 4-year-olds and 3-year-olds were assigned tasks such as taking the mail out of the box or canceling stamps. Five-year-olds were responsible for reading the address and converting it into a village color dot so that the nonreaders could put the letter into the appropriate village box. As can be seen in these photographs, this process involved cooperation and teamwork. Without both cooperation and teamwork, the difficult job of sorting could not have been accomplished.

Narrative for Children	"After the mail was sorted by village, some of us had to sort it by room number. Sometimes some of us had to work during naptime. Sorting mail sure did take a long time! We worked hard together! On Thursdays, some of us delivered the mail."

Narrative for Adults	**Children can develop their own methods of accomplishing a task when given opportunities to make decisions.**

The first mail sorting experience was mainly organized and directed by Miss Shinkey and myself. However, the second and third times that the children sorted the mail were more child directed. With increasing independence in decision making, the children developed several shortcuts such as eliminating the color dot. In addition, the children traded jobs when individuals grew tired of a specific job. Finally, several younger children successfully moved into positions that involved reading the number or letter code, an accomplishment which greatly delighted me.

After working over an hour sorting mail, Curtisia commented, "We sure are working hard!"

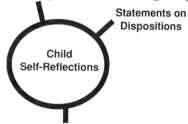

Statements on Dispositions

Child Self-Reflections

Our Mailbags

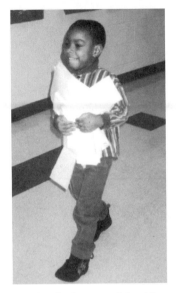

| "In the beginning, we did not have a mailbag. When some of us carried the mail, they dropped it all over the place. We decided to make a mailbag."

Indicators of Dispositions

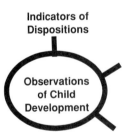

Observations of Child Development

Adam, the boy pictured above, shows his pride in this project by the expression on his face.

Narrative for Adults | **Children will work with purpose to fulfill a need that they recognize as being meaningful to them. Thus, their work has purpose and enhances their learning.**

The children did not realize that they would need a mailbag until they started to gather the mail from the villages. Almost all the mail carriers could be seen dropping mail as they walked back to the post office. That is when someone said that they needed a mailbag. Thus, the need was recognized and the work began to meet that need.

| Narrative for Children | "Tim, Karissa, Amber, and Brian researched mailbags in our books about mail. They decided to make a mailbag out of paper." |

Narrative for Adults OUR REFERENCE BOOKS. The children were exposed to and had access to several reference books pertaining to the mail system. They readily utilized these books to gain information on how to make the items that they needed, such as their mailbag. In addition, the books helped the children understand the mail sorting process. The children became very independent in their research and often initiated a search for information. This initiative in seeking knowledge is a lifeskill that will serve the children well throughout their lives.

Narrative for Children	"They drew a rectangle. Then, they cut it out and taped the edges together."

Narrative for Children	"Next, they made the handle. The first handle Karissa made was too short. The second handle

was too wide. Tim said that it needed to be longer."

Narrative for Children	"Karissa did not believe Tim. He showed Karissa the picture of the mailbag on the cover of the book."

Narrative for Children	"Finally, Karissa told Tim to draw the handle. Then she cut it out. This handle

was too narrow and tore. Miss Steinheimer showed Tim and Karissa how to use a yardstick to make a straight line for cutting."

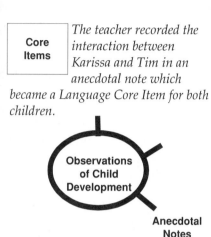

Core Items — *The teacher recorded the interaction between Karissa and Tim in an anecdotal note which became a Language Core Item for both children.*

Observations of Child Development

Anecdotal Notes

Narrative for Children | "Tim and Karissa made a long and wide handle. They taped it onto the top of the mailbag."

Narrative for Adults | **Children need opportunities to discuss and argue. Thus, they will gain in their ability to persuade and compromise, two very important social skills.**

Indicators of Dispositions | Karissa and Tim, two 4-year-olds, took on the job of creating a mailbag out of paper. This led to a lengthy interchange about the handle. Karissa drew a short handle using a picture on the cover of a book as her reference. Tim told her that it had to be bigger. Thus, Karissa drew a handle that was a little longer and wider. Tim told her that the handle was too fat. Karissa insisted that it would work and kept on cutting. Tim tried to convince Karissa that he needed the long strip on the edge of her paper. She did not agree and finished her cutting. Then, he showed her the picture on the book cover. Karissa kept on cutting. Next, she tried her handle on for size and discovered that it would not work. Therefore, she asked Tim to draw the handle. She cut out the long and narrow handle that he drew. It tore as she cut it out. However, they still thought that it would work after they cut it out. It did not. I gave them a yardstick and showed the pair how to draw a straight line with it. They made a long and wide handle for the bag which they attached to the bag with tape. After a trial run without mail, they were satisfied with their accomplishment.

Teacher Journal	**THE IMPORTANCE OF OBSERVATION AND TIMING.** Karissa and Tim benefited from the opportunity to discuss and

solve their own problem. They argued with purpose and invested energy in their argument. I observed their actions and discussion carefully. I carefully considered when and if my assistance would be needed. I decided that my assistance was not needed until the end when their narrow crooked handle tore repeatedly and a little frustration showed on their faces. That is when I taught them how to use a ruler to draw a straight line. They learned this new skill and successfully completed their task. It is very important that adults observe children in order to see when and if their intervention is needed. In addition to timing, the amount of guidance needs to be considered. Children become independent in their thinking only when given opportunities to do so as Karissa and Tim had here.

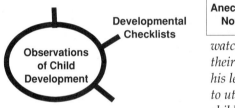

Brian, as a 3-year-old, felt comfortable watching the older children complete their task. He was able to participate at his level and was proud that he was able to utilize the techniques that the older children were using.

The teacher recorded her observations on the Work Sampling Developmental Checklist.

Personal Social Development Domain *(Approach to Learning)*	Not yet ☐
C 3. Approaches tasks with flexibility and inventiveness.	In process ☐
	Proficient ☐

Individualized Items	Brian, a child who began as part of the mailbag con-struction team, chose to leave the team as the discussion

became more intense. Brian did not go very far and began to work on his own mailbag beside Karissa and Tim. He observed the techniques that they were using and applied them to his own mailbag. In the end, he had created his own mailbag complete with a flap that opened. Brian, a 3-year-old, benefited from being exposed to a task that was being completed by older children. He participated at the level that he was comfortable with and was able to utilize the techniques that the older children were using.

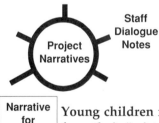

| Narrative for Children | "The mail fell out of our paper mailbag. After some discussion, we decided to try something else." |

| Narrative for Children | "Tim made a mailbag out of a cardboard box. The mail did not fall out of this mailbag. However, the |

mail carriers said that this bag was too heavy. It took two people to carry it! We had to try something else."

Project Narratives — **Staff Dialogue Notes**

The teacher and associate teacher discussed the children's frustration and progress through the problem-solving process. A decision was made to continue letting them solve the problem but to assist by introducing fabric to the children.

| Narrative for Adults | **Young children need opportunities to experiment and learn from their "mistakes."** |

The children created their first mailbag out of paper and tape. When they discovered it would not hold the mail, Tim suggested that they try a cardboard box. The mail carriers reported that it was too heavy and that it took two people to carry it. This led to a need for a stronger, lighter material. At my suggestion, the children used fabric to make the final mailbag. This process took several days and involved several children reflecting on their own work as well as the work of others. With each reflection came another solution and greater success!

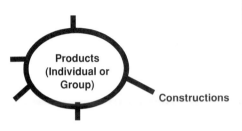

| Narrative for Children | "Miss Steinheimer suggested that we make our mailbag out of fabric. Andy, Tim, Brian, and Amber decided to make this mailbag. First, they drew a line for cutting. Then, they used Miss Steinheimer's big scissors to cut on the line." |

| Narrative for Children | "Next, they sewed the bag together using a needle and yarn. Andy and Amber made sure the mail would not fall |

out of the bottom of the bag. They also made a handle for the mailbag."

| Child Self-Reflections | Narrative for Children | "Tim painted U. S. Mail on our bag. This mailbag |

worked well. The mail did not fall out. It could be carried by one or two people."

Children need opportunities to interact with experts.

| Narrative for Children | "We showed our mailbag to Mr. Tim, the mail carrier, who came to visit. He thought that our

mailbag was as good as his mailbag."

Mr. Tim, the mail carrier, came to school to tell the children about his job. In addition, he showed them his equipment and mail truck. On the day before his visit, the children and I formulated a list of questions to ask him. This was a difficult task for all of us. However, this preparation helped the children ask Mr. Tim many meaningful questions. The children also reported on their mailbag and postal system to Mr. Tim. Finally, the children had a chance to observe Mr. Tim's mail truck, which led to the creation of their own mail truck.

| Teacher Journal | **LEARNING HOW TO FORMULATE QUESTIONS.** Compiling a list of questions to ask Mr. Tim, the mail carrier, was a difficult task for my children. We worked hard at discerning the difference between a question and a statement. In addition, the children would get stuck on a specific topic such as the color of his truck and needed encouragement to move on to another topic. However, our struggle produced a list of about 10 questions that the children successfully asked Mr. Tim on the day of his visit. In addition, they asked many spontaneous relevant questions during his visit. This was our first interview with an expert.

Verbal
Language

Products
(Individual or Group)

Formulating questions relevant to a topic during a discussion is a difficult task for young children. However, my class has increased tremendously in their ability to formulate and ask questions. In fact, during our discussion about what questions we would ask at the post office, the children contributed many intriguing questions. Thus, their growth in the skill of questioning was very apparent to all of us.

Our Mail Truck

| Narrative for Adults | Young children are capable of investigating topics in order to gain information |

that is meaningful to them. Teaching them investigating skills helps them to become confident learners.

The children investigated mail trucks before beginning construction of their own mail truck. In this process, they observed and sat in a real mail truck, looked at pictures taken during that experience, and looked for pictures of mail trucks in books. The children used all of these experiences to create drawings needed in order to construct their own mail truck. Thus, their investigation was meaningful to them, and they went about it with great purpose.

| Narrative for Children | "First, we looked at Mr. Tim's mail truck." |

| Pictures | Narrative for Children | "We also looked for pictures of mail trucks in books. Some of |

us drew pictures of the front, sides, and back of our mail truck."

| Narrative for Children | "Some of us taped all of our drawings and photographs onto our mail truck planning board." |

Young children can use measuring techniques in ways that are meaningful to them. In addition, they can learn how to record measurements so that the data can be used by others.

Developmental Checklists **Core Items** Karissa and Michael used plastic pegs to measure the front, back, and sides of the trike which would be transformed into a mail truck. As they completed each measurement, they wrote it onto their measurement sheet. These labeled drawings were used by other children to measure the cardboard needed for the truck.

Narrative for Children "Next, some of us measured our mail truck and wrote the measurements onto our measuring chart."

Narrative for Children "Some of us measured and cut the cardboard for our mail truck. Our measuring chart told them how big to cut the pieces."

Narrative for Adults Teaching children to use a variety of tools in different ways empowers them.

During the construction of the mail truck, the children learned how to use a variety of tools to perform tasks. For instance, several children learned how to use a ruler to draw a straight line at a certain measurement. In addition, several children learned how to carefully score cardboard with scissors before cutting it to make cutting easier. Also, the children learned how to use pipe cleaners to attach materials together. Thus, the children have added these skills to their repertoire and will be able to use them in later projects independently.

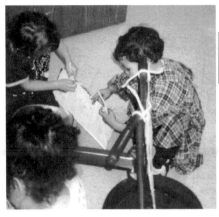

Narrative for Adults

USING CHILDREN'S DRAWINGS AS A REFERENCE FOR PAINTING. The children used their drawings of the truck to paint the details onto the cardboard. They repeatedly referred to their drawings as they drew the details onto the cardboard using pencil. Then, they referred to the drawings again as they selected their paint and did the actual painting. Thus, their original drawings were used several times to complete several different tasks. The need to draw for a specific purpose and repeatedly referring to their drawings helps children understand the need for careful observation and attention to details as they draw.

Core Items	Narrative for Children

"Some of us painted our cardboard pieces white just like the color of a mail truck. When the white paint was dry, some of us drew the stripes onto the cardboard. Then, some of us painted them like the stripes on Mr. Tim's mail truck. Finally, some of us tied the cardboard pieces onto our mail truck."

Constructions	Narrative for Children

"Our mail truck worked well. Here is a picture of it in action!"

Our Mailbox Study

Narrative for Children	"First, we did our homework. Amber and Ryan typed a survey sheet onto the computer. We had to find out what kind of mailboxes each of us has. We looked at pictures of different mailboxes in our post office books. We discovered

some people do not have a mailbox. They have a mail slot."

Narrative for Adults	**Young children can and will amaze you if you let them.**

Teacher Journal	Several children worked on the computer to create a book about mailboxes. In order to do this, they had to type in each letter as shown on the story board (form used for children's

story dictation). This was not an easy task since they had to convert most letters from lower case as it appears on this page to upper case as it appears on the keyboard, and back to lower case as it appears on the screen. In addition, the children learned how to use the shift key for upper case letters, spacebar for spaces between words, and a beginning awareness of commas and periods. The children's book about mailboxes represents several hours of intense work on the computer. Thus, the children strengthened their ability to persist in completing a difficult task.

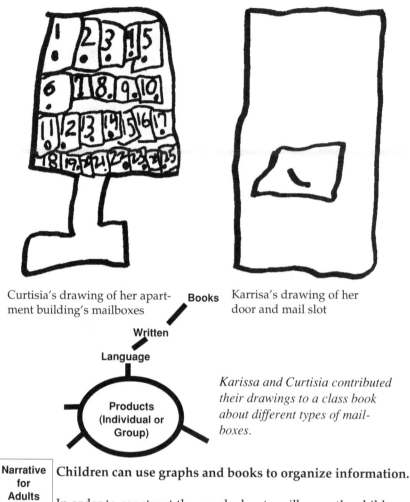

Curtisia's drawing of her apartment building's mailboxes

Books

Karrisa's drawing of her door and mail slot

Written

Language

Products (Individual or Group)

Karissa and Curtisia contributed their drawings to a class book about different types of mailboxes.

Narrative for Adults

Core Items

Children can use graphs and books to organize information.

In order to construct the graph about mailboxes, the children did several things. First, they did some investigation which included completing a mailbox survey and investigating different types of mailboxes found in our post office books. The children then drew a picture of each type of mailbox for their chart headings. Next, each child had to write his or her name on an envelope and place it under the picture of the mailbox most similar to his or her mailbox. The children then totaled each column and wrote the total onto the chart. After this was done, they were asked to analyze the data. This graph served as the basis for the book about mailboxes.

Narrative for Children	"Miss Crider let some of us put her new mailbox together. We used it in our living center for a few days."

Narrative for Adults
Teacher Journal

THANKS FOR THE HELP. During our mail project, we received help from a variety of sources. For example, Miss Crider, a teacher next door to our room, let us use her new mailbox. Another teacher let us borrow some stamps. In addition, we received help from other teachers in our building, our families who contributed items for us to use for our project, and experts who shared their knowledge with us. It is important that children realize that they can depend on others outside their immediate circle to help them learn and grow. The children were able to realize this during our mail project through the help that we received.

Our Stamp Study

Narrative for Children	"We looked at many different types of real stamps. We found out that most stamps have pictures, words, and numbers on them. We wrote about our stamps."

Core Items	Narrative for Children	"We made our own stamps. First, we drew a picture. Next, we

made copies of our drawings. The copy machine made little copies of our drawings about the same size as stamps. Then, we cut out our stamps. Finally, each of us put one stamp on a page for our stamp album, took one stamp home to keep, and used one stamp to mail a letter to his or her pen pal."

Narrative for Adults	**Children benefit from experiences with real collections of objects.**

After several weeks of freely exploring a collection of stamps, the children were asked to select some stamps for the class stamp album. I asked the children to select up to three stamps that were alike in some way. After attaching the stamps to their individual page, they wrote about their stamps.

On the following day, I asked the children to create their own stamp for the album. They talked about what they wanted to draw, drew their pictures, and then "shrunk" their drawing to the size of stamps using the photocopy machine.

Our Envelope Study

Narrative for Children

"Some of us sorted our envelopes by size. Then, they glued or taped them onto their charts. Some of us measured each envelope and cut strips of paper the length and width of each envelope. Then, some of us counted each square on a strip and wrote down the measurements. Lastly, some of us wrote some words on our chart. They wrote down which envelope was the smallest and which was the largest. We helped each other with our writing."

Narrative for Adults

Dealing with a shortage of materials or equipment can help young children learn how to share and improvise.

Indicators of Dispositions

Three pairs of children worked on seriating and measuring envelopes for graphs. They had available to them two brushes, two pots of glue, and one tape dispenser. Thus, the teams had to decide which teams would use what to attach their envelopes to their charts. In addition, each team had to work out who would use the tape or glue within their team. All teams successfully completed this task in spite of the shortage of materials and equipment.

Anecdotal Notes	Narrative for Adults

I DID IT MY WAY. Each of the children approached the task of measuring the envelopes in a different way. For example, Amber would lay a strip of graph paper down along the envelopes edge and cut off the extra paper on both ends. Andy started his strip even with one of the envelope's edges and cut off the other end of the strip to match the length or width of the envelope. Karissa felt comfortable with taking several little pieces and piecing them together to make the length that she needed. And Michael made a strip for every side of his envelope! All of these techniques worked and showed the diversity of the children's thinking.

Narrative for Adults

Children can teach each other new skills when given opportunities to do so.

Tim, who is a very capable copywriter, worked with Andy to create their graph. He encouraged and taught Andy how to recognize and write several letters. Both children grew from this experience.

Developmental Checklists	Narrative for Adults

CONCENTRATION! The task of making a chart of envelopes seriated by size was a difficult one for the children. They worked on this task for around two hours without any loss of interest. In addition, the children had to work in the hallway due to a lack of space in our room. Thus, they had to deal with distractions such as people walking around and sometimes on their work. Even though the children had to deal with the difficulty of the task, the shortage of materials, and the outside distractions, the children successfully completed their task. In addition, they learned or in some cases perfected many new skills such as measuring with graph paper, recording measurements, seriating by size, and copywriting. They amazed me!

Our Post Office Field Trip

Narrative for Adults

TRANSFER OF SKILLS. Tonise used a tracing skill to make postal carrier hats. She learned this skill during a previous project experience in which she used a pattern to make birthday hats. She was able to transfer her knowledge of this skill in order to independently make postal worker hats for her classmates.

Individualized Items	Narrative for Children

"We saw many different types of mail. We saw lots of machines. We saw how the postal workers sort the mail. When we got back to our school, we made mail carrier hats."

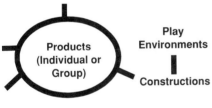

Products (Individual or Group)

Play Environments

Constructions

Narrative for Children

"We sorted the mail. We delivered the mail to mailboxes in our room."

Teacher Journal	Narrative for Adults

NOW THAT IS INTEREST! The children's continued interest in this project has amazed me. The project lasted for 6 weeks of in-depth study. In addition, the children's focus amazed me. For example, one day we were busy talking with some firefighters who visited our school for a fire safety program. The firefighters showed us their equipment and truck. They also let the children sit in their truck. After the firefighters left, I thought for sure that the children would want to re-create the firefighters experience. Instead, during playtime, the children were busy re-creating their own version of the post office that we had visited the day before!

Our Project Reports

Captions	Narrative for Children	"First, Miss Steinheimer and Miss Shinkey took many photographs. We then put the photographs into order. Next, we told Miss Steinheimer what to write about each picture."

Books	Child Self-Reflections	Narrative for Children	"Some of us copied Miss Steinheimer's writing for each page. Then, we taped the photographs onto paper to make the pages for our book.

Now we know how to make books, and we made some about how we made our mailbags, mail truck, and our post office."

| Narrative for Adults | Young children benefit from opportunities to create books about what they have experienced. |

At the end of our mail project, I suggested that we make a book about each of the major things that we had done. The children sorted photographs for our books, helped put the photographs into sequential order, and dictated what they wanted to say about each group of photographs. Then I wrote their words on sticky notes and attached the notes to the pictures for each page. Next, some of the 4-year-olds spent some time copying the text onto cards for the book while some of the 3-year-olds assembled each page. This whole process helped the children review what they had accomplished and learned. In addition, the book served as a report for others to share in their accomplishment.

Our Open House

Letters	Verbal Language	Narrative for Children

"We invited our pen pals from Green 1 over to our room to learn about our mail project. We sent our pen pals invitations to our open house. When our pen pals came, we told them about our mail project. We all had something to share!"

Narrative for Adults   A child needs several opportunities to reflect, evaluate, and report on his/her own growth in knowledge. This process enhances a child's disposition for learning and helps the child to realize his or her own growth. In addition, others have an opportunity to learn about the subject that the child is reporting on.

Statements on Dispositions   During an open house, Karissa explained in detail how a letter gets from one place to another. She used a written flow chart that she helped create as her reference. After this experience, Karissa commented on her reporting experience. Her pride in her accomplishment was evident to all.

APPENDIX

Overview of the
Work Sampling System

THE WORK SAMPLING DOMAINS

The Work Sampling System is based on seven categories or *domains*, each of which is composed of several *functional components* and *performance indicators*. Each of the domains is carried across all three elements of the System. The seven domains are:

1. **Personal and Social Development.** This domain has a dual focus. First, it refers to children's feelings about themselves. The teacher can learn about these feelings by observing children, listening to their comments, and hearing families talk about their children. Included in this focus are indicators that refer to children's views of themselves as learners and their sense of responsibility to themselves and others. The second focus concerns children's social development, including their interaction with peers and adults. Particularly important to this domain are the skills children show they are acquiring while making friends, solving conflicts, and functioning effectively in groups.
2. **Language and Literacy.** This domain emphasizes the acquisition of language skills to convey and interpret meaning. All of the components integrate multiple skills, rather than isolated abilities. The indicators in this domain reflect the belief that children learn to read and write the same way they learn to speak—naturally and slowly, using increasingly accurate approximations of adult norms.
3. **Mathematical Thinking.** Mathematics is about patterns and relationships, and about seeking multiple solutions to problems. The focus of this domain is on children's approaches to mathematical thinking and problem solving. Emphasis is placed on how students acquire and use strategies to perceive, understand, and act on mathematical problems. The content of mathematics (concepts and procedures) is stressed, but within the larger context of understanding and application (knowing and doing).

4. **Scientific Thinking.** This domain addresses ways of thinking and inquiring about the natural and physical world. Emphasized are the processes of scientific investigation, because process skills are embedded in and fundamental to all science instruction and content. The focus of this domain is on how children actively investigate through observing, recording, describing, questioning, forming explanations, and drawing conclusions.

5. **Social Studies.** This domain emphasizes the acquisition of social and cultural understanding. Children acquire this understanding from personal experience and by learning about the experiences of others. As children study present-day and historical topics, they gain understanding of human interdependence and the relationships between people and the environment.

6. **The Arts.** The emphasis in this domain is on children's engagement with the arts (dance, dramatics, music, and art), both actively and receptively. The components address how children use the arts to express, represent, and integrate their experiences, ideas, and emotions, and how children develop an appreciation for the arts. Rather than emphasizing mastery of skills related to particular art forms, this domain focuses on how using and appreciating the arts enables children to demonstrate what they know and to expand their thinking.

7. **Physical Development.** The emphasis in this domain is on physical development as an integral part of children's well-being and ability to take advantage of educational opportunities. The components address gross motor skills, fine motor skills, and personal health and safety. A principal focus is on children's ability to move in ways that demonstrate control, balance, and coordination. Fine motor skills are equally important in laying the groundwork for artistic expression, handwriting, and self-care skills. Also included are children's growing competence to understand and manage their personal health and safety.

OBSERVING, COLLECTING, AND SUMMARIZING

The purpose of the Work Sampling System is to document and assess children's skills, knowledge, behavior, and accomplishments across a wide variety of classroom activities and areas of learning on multiple occasions. It consists of three complementary elements: 1) observations by teachers using Developmental Guidelines and Checklists, 2) collection of children's work in Portfolios, and 3) summaries of this information on Summary Reports.

One of the Work Sampling System's strengths is its systematic structure. It is based on collecting extensive information from multiple sources and using all of this information collectively to make evaluative decisions about what children know and can do. In its reliance on *observing, collecting,* and *summarizing,* Work Sampling organizes the assessment process so that it is both comprehensive in scope and manageable for teachers and students. Students are observed, information is collected, and performance is summarized on three occasions throughout the school year: fall, winter, and spring. The mechanisms of observing, collecting, and summarizing are as follows:

The *Developmental Guidelines* provide a framework for observation. They give teachers a set of observational criteria that are based on national standards and knowledge of child development. The guidelines set forth developmentally appropriate expectations for children at each age/grade level. In using the Guidelines as the basis of their professional judgements, teachers in different settings make decisions about children's behavior, knowledge, and accomplishments using identical criteria. Teachers' observations are recorded on the *Developmental Checklists.*

Portfolios are purposeful collections of children's work that illustrate children's efforts, progress, and achievements. These collections are intended to display the individual nature and quality of children's work and progress over time. Work Sampling advocates a structured approach to portfolio collection through the collection of two types of work samples: Core Items and Individualized Items. Core Items are designed to show growth over time, and the quality of work across the curriculum. Individualized Items are designed to portray the unique characteristics of the child and to reflect work that integrates many domains of curriculum. Both children and teachers are involved in the design, selection, and evaluation of the portfolios.

Summary Reports are completed three times a year. Teachers combine information from the Developmental Checklists and Portfolios with their own knowledge of child development to make evaluative decisions about student performance and progress. They summarize their knowledge of the child as they make ratings and write brief comments describing the student's strengths and identifying areas in need of development.

Work sampling not only provides the teacher with clear criteria for evaluation but also incorporates the teacher's expertise and judgment. An evaluation system that does not dictate curriculum or instructional methods, it is designed for use with diverse groups of children, in a variety of settings. The Work Sampling System is a flexible framework for assessment that helps teachers structure their assessments systematically and that encourages teachers to devise techniques best suited to their styles, their students, and the context within which they teach.

SUMMARY

The three elements of the Work Sampling System form an integrated whole. Checklists record a student's growth in relationship to teacher expectations and national standards. Portfolios graphically display the texture and quality of the child's work as well as his or her progress over time. Summary Reports integrate this information into a concise record that the student's family can understand and that administrators can use.

Work Sampling draws upon teachers' perceptions of students while informing, expanding, and structuring their observations. It assesses students' development and accomplishments—rather than test-taking skills—in meaningful, curriculum-based activities. It enables children's unique learning styles to be recognized and nurtured, instead of rigidly classifying them as high- or low-achievers based on narrow assessments. It enables both children and families to become actively involved in the assessment process. And, finally, by objectively documenting what children learn and how teachers teach, the Work Sampling System provides for meaningful evaluation and genuine accountability.

References

The American heritage dictionary (3rd ed.). (1994). Boston: Houghton Mifflin.

Berk, L., & Winsler, A. (1995). *Scaffolding children's learning: Vygotsky and early childhood education.* Washington, DC: National Association for the Education of Young Children.

Bodrova, E., & Leong, D. (1996). *Tools of the mind: The Vygotskian approach to early childhood education.* Englewood Cliffs, NJ: Prentice-Hall.

Bowers, A. (1995). *Portfolios for assessment and instruction.* Greensboro, NC: ERIC Clearinghouse on Counseling and Student Services.

Bredekamp, S. (Ed.). (1987). *Developmentally appropriate practice in early childhood programs serving children from birth through age 8* (Expanded ed.). Washington, DC: National Association for the Education of Young Children.

Bredekamp, S., & Copple, C. (Eds.). (1997). *Developmentally appropriate practice in early childhood programs serving children from birth through age 8* (Rev. ed.). Washington, DC: National Association for the Education of Young Children.

Bredekamp, S., & Rosegrant, T. (Eds.). (1992). *Reaching potentials: Vol. 1. Appropriate curriculum and assessment for young children.* Washington, DC: National Association for the Education of Young Children.

Bredekamp, S., & Rosegrant, T. (Eds.). (1995). *Reaching potentials: Vol. 2. Transforming early childhood curriculum and assessment.* Washington, DC: National Association for the Education of Young Children.

Bruner, J. (1996). *The culture of education.* Cambridge, MA: Harvard University Press.

Buzan, T., & Buzan, B. (1996). *The mind map book.* New York: Penguin Group.

Carter, S. (1996). *Integrity.* New York: Basic Books.

Chandler, R. (1997). *Raymond Chandler speaking* (D. Gardiner & K. S. Walker, Eds.). Berkeley: University of California Press.

Chard, S. (1994). *The project approach: A practical guide, I and II.* Edmonton: University of Alberta, Instructional Technology Center.

Children's Defense Fund (1995). *The state of America's children.* Washington, DC: Author.

Cohen, D. (1993, January 20). Assessment alternative for younger students seen honing teachers' skills, observation. *Education Week, 12,* pp. 6–7.

Cohen, D., Stern, V., & Balaban, N. (1997). *Observing and recording the behavior of young children* (4th ed.). New York: Teachers College Press.

Derman-Sparks, L. (1989). *Anti-bias curriculum: Tools for empowering young children.* Washington, DC: National Association for the Education of Young Children.

DeVries, R., & Kohlberg, L. (1990). *Constructivist early childhood education: Overview and comparison with other programs.* Washington, DC: National Association for the Education of Young Children.

Dichtelmiller, M., Jablon, J., Dorfman, A., Marsden, D., & Meisels, S. (1994). *Teacher's manual of the work sampling system.* Ann Arbor, MI: Rebus Planning Associates.

Edwards, C., Gandini, L., & Forman, G. (Eds.). (1993). *The hundred languages of children.* Norwood, NJ: Ablex.

Forman, G. (1994). *Different media, different languages.* In L. Katz & B. Cesarone (Eds.), Reflections on the Reggio Emilia approach (pp. 41–53). Urbana, IL: ERIC Clearinghouse on Elementary and Early Childhood Education.

Forman, G., Lee, M., Wrisley, L., & Langley, J. (1993). The city in the snow: Applying the multisymbolic approach in Massachusetts. In C. Edwards, L. Gandini, & G. Forman (Eds.), *The hundred languages of children* (pp. 233–250). Norwood, NJ: Ablex.

Gandini, L. (1993). Fundamentals of the Reggio Emilia approach to early childhood education. *Young Children, 49,* 4–8.

Gardner, H. (1983). *Frames of the mind.* New York: Basic Books.

Gardner, H. (1991). *The unschooled mind: How children think and how schools should teach.* New York: Basic Books.

Gardner, H. (1993). *Multiple intelligences: The theory in practice.* New York: Basic Books.

Goldhaver, G., Smith, D., & Sortino, S. (1996). Observing, recording, understanding: The role of documentation in early childhood teacher education. In J. Hendricks (Ed.), *First steps toward teaching the Reggio way* (pp. 198–209). Upper Saddle River, NJ: Prentice Hall.

Grace, C. (1992). *The portfolio and its use: Developmentally appropriate assessment of young children.* (ERIC Document Reproduction Service No. No. EDO-PS-11)

Gullo, D. F. (1994). *Understanding assessment and evaluation in early childhood education.* New York: Teachers College Press.

Hart, L. (1983). *Human brain and human learning.* Oak Creek, AZ: Books for Educators.

Hendricks, J. (Ed.). (1996). *First steps toward teaching the Reggio way.* Upper Saddle River, NJ: Prentice Hall.

Hills, T. (1992). Reaching potentials through appropriate assessment. In S. Bredekamp & T. Rosegrant (Eds.), *Reaching potentials: Vol. 1. Appropriate curriculum and assessment for young children* (pp. 43–63). Washington, DC: National Association for the Education of Young Children.

Howard, P. (1994). *The owner's manual for the brain.* Austin, TX: Leornian Press.

Jablon, J., Marsden, D., Meisels, S., & Dichtelmiller, M. (1994). *Omnibus guidelines: Preschool through third grade.* Ann Arbor, MI: Rebus Planning Associates.

Jalongo, M., (1991). The role of the teacher in the 21st century. Bloomington, IN:

National Educational Service.

Jensen, E. (1995). *Brain-based learning and teaching*. Del Mar, CA: Turning Point Publishing.

Jones, E. (Ed.). (1993). *Growing teachers: Partnerships in staff development*. Washington, DC: National Association for the Education of Young Children.

Kamii, C. (1982). *Number in preschool and kindergarten: Educational implications of Piaget's theory*. Washington, DC: National Association for the Education of Young Children.

Kamii, C., & Ewing, J. K. (1996). Basing teaching on Piaget's constructivism. *Childhood Education, 72*(5), 260–264.

Katz, L. (1985). *Dispositions in early childhood education*. ERIC/ECE Bulletin, 18(2), 1–3.

Katz, L. (1987). Early Education: What should young children be doing? In S. L. Kagan (Ed.), *The care and education of America's young children: Obstacles and opportunities* (90th Yearbook of the National Society for the Study of Education, Part I, pp. 50–68). Chicago: National Society for the Study of Education.

Katz, L. (1990). Impressions of Reggio Emilia preschools. *Young Children, 45*(6), 10–11.

Katz, L. (1995). *Talks with teachers of young children: A collection*. Norwood, NJ: Ablex.

Katz, L., & Chard, S. (1989). *Engaging children's minds: The project approach*. Norwood, NJ: Ablex.

Katz, L., & Chard, S. (1996). *The contribution of documentation to the quality of early childhood education*. Champaign, IL: ERIC Clearinghouse on Elementary and Early Childhood Education.

Keats, E. J. (1968). *A letter to Amy*. New York: Harper & Row.

Knapp, M. (Ed.). (1995). *Teaching for meaning in high-poverty classrooms*. New York: Teachers College Press.

Kotulak, R. (1993). Unlocking the mind [Series in the Chicago Tribune].

Kotulak, R. (1996). *Inside the brain: Revolutionary discoveries of how the mind works*. Kansas City, MO: Andrews & McMeel.

Lam, T. (1995). *Fairness in performance assessment*. Greensboro, NC: ERIC Clearinghouse on Counseling and Student Services.

Lynch, E., & Hanson, M. (1992). *Developing cross-cultural competence: A guide for working with young children and their families*. Baltimore, MD: Brookes.

Malaguzzi, L. (1993). History, ideas, and basic philosophy: An interview with Lella Gandini. In C. Edwards, L. Gandini, & G. Forman (Eds.), *The hundred languages of children* (pp. 41–89). Norwood, NJ: Ablex.

Mayesky, M. (1990). *Creative activities for young children*. Albany, NY: Delman.

Meisels, S. (1993). Remaking classroom assessment with the Work Sampling System. *Young Children, 48*, 34–40.

Meisels, S. J., Jablon, J. R., Marsden, D. B., Dichtelmiller, M. L., Dorfman, A. B., & Steele, D. M. (1994). *An overview: The Work Sampling System*. Ann Arbor, MI: Rebus Planning Associates.

Meisels, S., Liaw, F., Dorfman, A., & Fails, R. (1995). The Work Sampling System:

Reliability and validity of a performance assessment for young children. *Early Childhood Research Quarterly, 10*(3).

Merriam-Webster dictionary (5th ed.). (1994). Springfield, MA: Merriam-Webster.

Mills, R. (1989). Portfolios capture rich array of student performance. *The School Administrator, 47*(10), 8–11.

Morgan, T., & Thaler, S. (1996). *Capturing childhood memories.* New York: Berkeley Publishing Group.

National Board for Professional Teaching Standards. (1996). *Standards for early childhood/generalist certification. In Guidelines for the preparation of early childhood professionals.* Washington, DC: National Association for the Education of Young Children.

Neal, A. (1976). *Exhibits for the small museum: A handbook.* Nashville, TN: American Association for State and Local History.

Neal, A. (1986). *Help for the small museum: Handbook of exhibit ideas and methods.* Boulder, CO: Pruett.

New, R. (1990). Excellent early education: A city in Italy has it! *Young Children, 45*(6), 4–10.

New, R. (1991). Early childhood teacher education in Italy: Reggio Emilia's master plan for "master" teachers. *Journal of Early Childhood Teacher Education, 12*(37), 3.

Perrone, V. (1991). Association for Childhood Education International: Position paper on standardized testing. *Childhood Education, 67,* 131–142.

Rankin, B. (1992). Inviting children's creativity: A story of Reggio Emilia, Italy. *Child Care Information Exchange,* No. 85, 30–35.

Smith, F. (1990). *To think.* New York: Teachers College Press.

Stiggins, K. (1994). *Performance assessment.* Greensboro, NC: ERIC Clearinghouse on Counseling and Student Services.

Sylwester, Robert. (1995). *A celebration of neurons: An educator's guide to the human brain.* Alexandria, VA: Association for Supervision and Curriculum Development.

Vecchi, V. (1993). The role of the atelierista. In C. Edwards, L. Gandini, & G. Forman (Eds.), *The hundred languages of children* (pp. 119–127). Norwood, NJ: Ablex.

Vermont Department of Education. (1988). *Working together to show results: An approach to accountability for Vermont.* Montpelier, VT: Author.

Vermont Department of Education. (1989). *Vermont writing assessment: The portfolio.* Montpelier, VT: Author.

Vygotsky, L. S. (1978). *Mind in society: The development of higher mental processes* (M. Cole, V. John-Steiner, S. Scribner, & E. Souberman, Eds. & Trans.). Cambridge, MA: Harvard University Press.

Wiggins, G. (1990). *The case of authentic assessment.* Washington, DC: ERIC Clearinghouse on Tests, Measurements, and Evaluation.

Index

About the Authors

JUDY HARRIS HELM, Ed.D., began her career teaching first grade, then taught, directed, and designed early childhood programs and trained teachers. While a professor at Bradley University she served on the Task Force for the design of the Valeska Hinton Early Childhood Education Center, a state-of-the-art urban collaboration school. She eventually left the university and became Professional Development Coordinator for the school. She continues as consultant to the program and now assists other schools in integrating research and new methods through her consulting and training company, Best Practices, Inc. She is currently state President of the Illinois Association for the Education of Young Children and a contributor for *Early Childhood Today*. Dr. Helm completed her graduate studies at West Virginia University.

SALLEE BENEKE is Master Teacher and Consultant for the Illinois Valley Community College Early Childhood Education Program in Oglesby, Illinois. Active in early childhood education for over twenty years, Ms. Beneke has been a prekindergarten at-risk teacher, early childhood special education teacher, center director, and head teacher in several child care centers. She was Lead Teacher for the Valeska Hinton Early Childhood Education Center in Peoria, Illinois, when this study began. Sallee graduated from Cornell College, Mt. Vernon, Iowa, and is currently a graduate student at the University of Illinois.

KATHY STEINHEIMER is a teacher of 3- and 4-year-olds at the Valeska Hinton Early Childhood Education Center. She has worked in a variety of settings including private child care and hospital child care. She completed an undergraduate degree in accounting but found that her real love was working with children and after several years in child care continued her education, completing both elementary and early childhood certification requirements at Bradley University. Ms. Steinheimer has been especially interested in multi-age early childhood programs and the implementation of the project approach and has shared her insights with many teachers.